# innovation
# & Tradition

# ERUPTIONS
## New Thinking across the Disciplines

Erica McWilliam
*General Editor*

Vol. 21

PETER LANG
New York • Washington, D.C./Baltimore • Bern
Frankfurt am Main • Berlin • Brussels • Vienna • Oxford

# innovation
# & Tradition

## The Arts, Humanities and the Knowledge Economy

Jane Kenway
Elizabeth Bullen
Simon Robb

EDITORS

PETER LANG
New York • Washington, D.C./Baltimore • Bern
Frankfurt am Main • Berlin • Brussels • Vienna • Oxford

Library of Congress Cataloging-in-Publication Data

Innovation & tradition: the arts, humanities and the knowledge economy /
edited by Jane Kenway, Elizabeth Bullen, Simon Robb.
p. cm. — (Eruptions; v. 21)
Includes bibliographical references and index
1. Humanities—Information services. 2. Humanities—Technological innovations.
3. Information services industry. 4. Humanities—Economic aspects.
5. Humanities—Study and teaching (Graduate) 6. Arts and globalization.
7. Civilization, Modern—21st century. I. Kenway, Jane. II. Bullen,
Elizabeth. III. Robb, Simon. IV. Series.
AZ103.I55   001.3—dc22   2004001633
.ISBN 0-8204-7140-2
ISSN 1091-8590

Bibliographic information published by **Die Deutsche Bibliothek**.
**Die Deutsche Bibliothek** lists this publication in the "Deutsche
Nationalbibliografie"; detailed bibliographic data is available
on the Internet at http://dnb.ddb.de/.

Cover design by Lisa Barfield

Cover art by Patricia Piccinini, *Protein Lattice*, Subset Red 1997
digital C type photograph 80 × 80 cm

The paper in this book meets the guidelines for permanence and durability
of the Committee on Production Guidelines for Book Longevity
of the Council of Library Resources.

© 2004 Peter Lang Publishing, Inc., New York
275 Seventh Avenue, 28th Floor, New York, NY 10001
www.peterlangusa.com

Printed in the United States of America

# CONTENTS

# ACKNOWLEDGMENTS

We wish to express our gratitude to the Australian Research Council which funded the three year Discovery-Project study, *Knowledge, Economy, Society: A Sociological Study of an Education Policy Discourse in Australia in Globalising Circumstances*. This book stems from that project and from the "New Generations" public forum, workshop, and seminar developed around the theme of the arts and humanities in the knowledge economy. We would like to thank the Hawke Research Institute and its Director, Professor Alison Mackinnon, for the support they provided for these activities. We are also grateful for the support of the Centre for Studies in Literacy, Policy and Learning Cultures and the Division of Education, Arts and Social Sciences, University of South Australia. We also express our appreciation for the generous contributions to our deliberations of Heather Kerr, Adelaide University, and Fiona Magowan, Adelaide University. We would like to thank Paul Carter and Patricia Piccinini for their kind permission to reproduce their images. Finally, we thank Kate Leeson, Editor, Hawke Research Institute, for copyediting.

# NOTE ABOUT THE COVER

The cover features "Protein Lattice—Subset Red" (1997) by Australian artist Patricia Piccinini. This image engages with fundamental issues to do with the limits of technology—how far should technology intrude into spheres of life that are traditionally non-technological? The rat with the ear is a product of capital investment in the innovative technologies. The image raises questions about the ethical and epistemological consequences of the developments in science and technology promoted via discourses associated with the knowledge economy. Like Piccinini's image, the essays in this collection raise critical questions about the limits of science, technology, innovation and commercialization in higher education and research, specifically in relation to the consequences of knowledge economy policies for the arts and humanities.

Patricia Piccinini (1997) "Protein Lattice—Subset Red" digital C type photograph 80 × 80 cm.

# ·1·

*Simon Robb & Elizabeth Bullen*

---

# A PROVOCATION

*Satire is the literary art of diminishing a subject by making it ridiculous and evoking toward it attitudes of amusement, contempt, indignation or scorn.*
(ABRAMS, 1981, P. 167)

*The Minister for Education in the UK has recently said that while he doesn't mind a few medievalists in the country, he cannot see why their choice of career should be funded by the state. He intends to get tough on "useless subjects."*
(GAITA, 2003, P. 11)

In the global knowledge economy, research and learning in the arts and humanities is a luxury. The so-called contributions of the arts and humanities to intellectual freedom, critical analysis, ethical debates, and identity are, within the new dispensation, only valuable when and if they can contribute to a system of commercialization and knowledge management. Consequently the arts and humanities find themselves marginal to major policy statements on the knowledge economy (see, for example, Commonwealth of Australia, 2001) and the development of research priorities nationally and internationally (see, for example, European Commission, 2002).

Any discipline, if it wishes to flourish in a knowledge economy, must bring to the table a knowledge that can contribute to the innovation system. What we mean by this is that it must bring a knowledge that can generate income. It must develop a knowledge that is economically inflected, grounded, if you like, in the ever-changing ebbs and flows of a global market. Innovation is not simply discovering new ideas; it is about developing those ideas so that they can be sold. It is about the economic essence of knowledge. It is about knowledge having an economic essence that needs to be discovered, understood, and expressed. Each discipline must inevitably produce not just knowledge but types of personalities capable of developing and delivering that knowledge to a global market. The personality that is most able to enact this process is the entrepreneur, one whose job it is to realize the potential value in any product or service. A knowledge economy needs bodies of knowledge and personalities appropriate to the innovation system and we can find these most obviously in the disciplines of science, technology, enterprise, and management.

We, the Committee for the Extermination of Arts and Humanities Funding in Higher Education, note with approval the current situation within institutions of higher education, where learning for its own sake has become an extravagance that increasingly few students can afford—or even want—and which disciplines in the humanities and creative arts are increasingly unable to provide. Scholars are less able to fulfil such traditional notions of the humanities as the preservation of knowledge "for its own sake" and the recovery of "lost" knowledge. These pursuits are, quite rightly, "perceived as past-directed" and "interest-driven" and are not amenable to the "methods-and-outcomes criteria applied to applications by research-funding bodies" (Ruthven, 1998, p. 98). We are gratified that some humanities scholars are beginning to realize that supporting a pursuit of the "life of the mind" indicates a "bunker-like mentality" (Cooper, 2002). Yet all too often we see the humanist prevaricate, trapped between wanting to appear to be someone who is in love with truth, a philosopher, but also a professional, with a career, as someone who does not want to appear too neurotic or precious (Gaita, 2002, p. 96).

Why indeed does your typical humanities scholar have such difficulty in coming to terms with the real world thinking of a knowledge economy? Surely those in the humanities realize that even the key figures of postmodernity acknowledge the centrality of the economy (Jameson, 1991; Harvey, 1989) and technology (Lyotard, 1993, 1984; Baudrillard, 1975) in these post-industrial times. Of course, perhaps this is not symptomatic of ignorance or a disinclination to understand one's own disciplinary perspectives. We acknowledge that the average humanities scholar has better things to do than spend their time laboring over Marxist detritus. The Committee is aware of, and commends, the humanist's dedication to productivity in terms of teaching, preparing research applications, administration, and generating research publications. We particularly congratulate those—sadly few—who have stopped the hand-wringing and recognized the wealth of entrepreneurial opportunities that a techno-economic approach to the arts and humanities affords. They are now making a contribution to the gross domestic product, our global competitiveness, and the national interest. That is the whole point of the entrepreneurial personality. Let us explain the economic logic behind this.

Any cursory reading of national, international, and supranational policy, not to mention *Business Week*, *The Financial Review*, or *Time* magazine for that matter, would tell the humanities scholar that we are living in a new knowledge society/information economy/information society/network society/ knowledge-based economy/new economy/learning economy/information age. As the OECD (1996, p. 7) tells us, "knowledge, especially technological knowledge, is the main source of economic growth and improvements in the quality of life." Knowledge is transformed into an economic object or applied to economic activities through the innovation process, making innovation (and competition) fundamental to economic growth. Humanists would do well to acquaint themselves with innovation research of the 1980s and in particular evolutionary economic theory (Nelson & Winter, 1982), the techno-economic paradigm identified by Freeman and Perez (1988) and Perez (1985), and new growth theory (Romer 1990, 1994). Both neoclassical and evolutionary schools are indebted to Schumpeter (1934, 1939). Schumpeter described innovation as a means to create a legal monopoly. Legal competitive advantage is reinforced by patent law which enables invention to be secured for sole exploitation through commercialization—in other words, the innovation process. In addition, Schumpeter identified the key role of the entrepreneur in economic growth. An innovative economy needs an army of entrepreneurs.

The humanities scholar needs to take some lessons from the real world if the Committee is to concede a possible utility for the arts and humanities. This would mean a number of things. Firstly, it would mean responding to, and working with, industry and commerce. If the humanist has concerns over the future of basic and curiosity-driven research and researcher autonomy in the disciplines more generally, they should be reassured by OECD (1996, p. 26) research which reminds us that some of the most important insights have come from the solution of industrial problems. Secondly, it would mean adapting to the reality that ideas and advances in science and technology are the drivers of economic growth and that if we do not invest in them we will not have sufficient knowledge workers to sustain wealth creation into the century. It is for this reason that the U.S. House of Representatives passed the *Technology Talent Act 2001*, an Act to help increase the number of people holding engineering, mathematics, science, and technology degrees. It is for this reason that the Commonwealth of Australia's innovation strategy (2001) includes a five-year funding package worth $2.9 billion for science and technology innovation and research (with an estimated business and research organization expenditure of $6 billion). Apologists for the humanities and creative arts seem to forget that the national and global good is at stake here. They need to focus on discovering ways in which to contribute to progress in the key growth areas like nanotechnology, biotechnology, and information technology. Thirdly, they need to think entrepreneurially and, to do this, the humanist needs to learn to think outside the square; to think creatively.

Here we think it wise to be precise about what creativity means in a knowledge economy. Creativity is the application of problem-solving skills and the ability to manage the production of ideas within a commercial framework. Creativity is a skill that is required by employers to fulfil industry goals; it is the application of managerial skills required within an industry context to facilitate industry growth. Creativity is a form of managerialism, which is required for creative industries. It is difficult to differentiate between this notion of creativity and the notion of entrepreneurialism. The entrepreneur and the creator are interchangeable, and we are aware of the exquisite semantic serendipity of this. This is the type of equivalence possible within a knowledge economy. We are confident that creativity coopted in this way has no disruptive critical value; it has only a material or economic value. The creative personality is produced within and works within a network of instruments and rationalities designed to maximize profit. The aim here is to minimize any risk from investing in creativity.

Once the humanist has learnt this lesson they would then be able, for example, to manage and facilitate entrepreneurial industry applications in the total quality management of critical and theoretical advertising, knowledge theme parks, interdisciplinary industrial knowledge, commercial creativity and diverse practical skills for virtual employers, interdisciplinary leisure projects, real world multimedia environments, and creative entrepreneurial industry arts. They would be able to develop innovative educational programs and research projects: "Nanotechnology in Shakespeare"; "Petrarch or protons?"; "Genomics, phenomics, and feminism." The lesson that the humanist should never forget is that creativity serves only one master, the economy, and that to serve that master creativity must attend to the needs of industry.

This is the potential for the arts and humanities. But what have they brought so far to the knowledge economy in terms of bodies of knowledge and personality? What evidence is there that the arts and humanities understand the economic essence of knowledge or the entrepreneurial personality? Perhaps a few examples may be illuminating. Let us take a look at some of the wisdom with which the humanities discuss an economic essence. We have Lyotard's (1993) "libidinal economy," the "gift economy" of Mauss (1967), Bataille (1988), and Derrida (1995) or the "poetic economics" as discussed in, for example, Shell (1982) or Heinzelman (1980). Here we see arguments about economics as a linguistic effect, an affect of desire, or a system founded on an unrepresentable excess of irrationality. Here we see "knowledge" that can only give in secret, as sacrifice; one that is as remote as possible from that of commerce, and indeed one that is close to death (Derrida, 1995). What are we to make of this unrepresentable presence within a knowledge economy, a presence that we see not only in a libidinal economy, but also in the irrational expenditure of a gift economy? How can these forces, which supposedly complicate the norm of "reciprocity" (Osteen & Woodmansee, 1999), and which are so incommensurate with logic and rationality, be represented, other than in the collapse of rationality, in the destruction of sense making, in the delirious apocalypse of all systems of exchange?

Likewise, in the same vein of disruption and chaos, we have humanists who argue that economies are "within" language, and that language is "within" economies, and that consequently an economy can be thought of in terms of an "aesthetic practice" (Shell, 1982; Heinzelman 1980, cited in Osteen & Woodmansee 1999). These then are typical contributions made by the humanities to an economic epistemology and quite clearly they are examples of the sheer irrelevance of the humanities to an understanding of a knowledge economy. These minor examples represent a much greater malaise, the inability of the humanities to accept that at the heart of all knowledge is an economic essence.

If we sweep away the valueless and trivial ephemera of humanities "knowledge," what personality type do we see being constructed? We see, in essence, a series of practices, both at the level of the classroom and of the researcher's page, for self-problematization through aesthetic means (Hunter, 1992). We see a series of practices devoted to the development of "taste." We have here a process of ongoing scrutiny (one that is aiming for ever more refined moments), oscillating between a subjective excess (of commonsense, emotionality, desire) and an objective restraint (disciplinary knowledge) (Hunter, 1992). The Committee would like to remind the reader that this process was born from German Romanticism and had at its core the aim of reconciling alienated or fragmented parts of "man," and of reconciling "man's" fragmented or alienated relationship to all spheres of life, including politics and the economy, not just aesthetic objects (Hunter, 1992). Individuals "constitute themselves as subjects of political experience by construing political events as symptoms of the same fundamental divisions of the 'ethical substance' that afflict them personally" (Hunter, 1992, pp. 353–354).

The economy, if we are to draw out an example that is useful for our analysis, is "problematized" as a site of rationality and desire, fragmentation and wholeness, ignorance and enlightenment. Likewise, and at the same time, the personality of the researcher is problematized in the same way, and the economy is the means through which this conflicted personality is "diagnosed." What we have here is a simultaneous contemplation of the self and the text and, in this case, a problematization of "knowledge," "economy," and "self."

Just as with any economy, there is a problematization that involves value, equivalence, and an exchange. What we have here is a necessarily disengaged, "non-rational" version of enlightenment (Hunter, 1992). What becomes obvious then, at least to this Committee, is that the aesthetic personality, opposed as it is towards instrumental reason, cannot engage with an economy in any way other than by being oppositional to commercialization and entrepreneurialism. Once practically engaged, aesthetic scepticism, that almost schizophrenic oscillation between incommensurable knowledge systems, will be compromised or destroyed by instrumental reason. Mundane knowledge within this system (instrumental reason) is "ethically worthless" (Hunter, 1992, p. 354). The corollary of this argument is that humanities knowledge, too, is economically worthless, as are its pedagogies and the subjects produced thereby.

Let us summarize these points. The technologies of an aesthetic personality require a constant and ever more refined oscillation between contrary systems of knowledge and identity. The (tragic) aim is either to reconcile these forces in some sort of "pleasing", or enlightening manner, or to abandon any notion of "aim" and instead commit to the process itself. This process needs to take place disengaged from an environment that demands the constant application of instrumental reason, utility, and law (government, for example). Why, the Committee asks, should the state fund what amounts to a neo-Romantic finishing school committed to an antagonistic relationship to the economy? Why should the state fund the development of a "taste" antithetical to practical innovations in knowledge, or, in other words, to a knowledge economy?

As one of the fathers of the knowledge economy, Peter F. Drucker (1993, p. 197), says, the problem with the liberal arts and the new humanities (that "motley crew" of "deconstructionists," "radical feminists," and "antiwesterners") is that "Instead of uniting [they] fragment." They fail because they do not integrate knowledge, because they do not create that "'univers[al] discourse' without which there can be no civilization" (Drucker, 1993, p. 197), a discourse we believe the knowledge economy can provide. The humanities fail because they fail to recognize that the future, "[i]ts material civilization and its knowledges rest on Western foundations: science; tools and technology; production; economics; money, finance and banking" (1993, p. 194).

This Committee has no problems with the aesthetic personality *per se*; if the market can support finishing schools that can supply this type of service, well and good. But if the aesthetic personality is irreconcilable to the world of engaged practice, if it is committed to useless knowledge and a valueless economy, we see no reason for its continued presence within the state-sponsored quest for innovation, entrepreneurship, commercialization, and innovation. The Committee has, so far, been unable to see any reason why it should support the valueless pursuits of the arts and humanities, their thoroughly anti-entrepreneurial stance, their feeble mimicry of "creativity," their so-called aesthetic knowledge, their romantic love of the sublime, and their juvenile obsessions with semantic eruptions. Word salad will not feed the poor.

The Committee on the other hand is an advocate for a rational knowledge economy. For the benefit of the troubled humanist we will rehearse our convictions briefly. "Knowledge," we argue, is the key factor in a competitive global economy network of communication and learning that is spread throughout and between industries for a national economy to thrive across all industries and related government sectors and within each organization describing a commercial potential knowledge economy and entrepreneurial spirit within all industries and sectors participating in the ongoing learning economy to thrive in the knowledge economy network of innovation that exists between ideas and the entrepreneurial spirit in globalized times to facilitate the growth of research and education communication commercialization deemed to be of importance to an innovative economy and an entrepreneurial spirit of stobie poles, Post-it notes, stump-jump ploughs, and atom bombs.

As things stand, arts and humanities research and education contribute nothing to a knowledge economy. They are valueless as ends in themselves and will assume value only when oriented to an overarching commercialization, managerial, and innovation strategy. This is a potential to which creative industries programs point, but the test of the true value of research in disciplines like English, cultural studies, and history ultimately rests on tangible outcomes and real (economic) benefits. Aesthetic knowledge and the aesthetic personality need, in the final instance, to accommodate themselves to the imperatives of commercializing and managing that knowledge within a market economy. The humanities must concede that the model of knowledge and personality most suitable to a knowledge economy is knowledge of the market and the personality of the entrepreneur. In this we can see the idea of innovation mapped onto programs for the production of knowledge and of personality. Aesthetic knowledge and the aesthetic personality need to bend to the "whole-person" imperatives of a globalized knowledge economy. If they do not, they will be wiped away. They will eke out their dying days in anachronistic finishing schools and museums of aesthetic deportment.

## References

Abrams, M. (1981). *A glossary of literary terms*, 4th ed. New York: CBS Publishing.
Bataille, G. (1988). *The accursed share: An essay on general economy. Vol. 1: Consumption*, trans. R. Hurley. New York: Zone Books (first published 1967).

Baudrillard, J. (1975). *The Mirror of production*. St Louis: Telos Press.

Commonwealth of Australia (2001). *Backing Australia's ability: An innovation action plan for the future*. Canberra: Commonwealth of Australia.

Cooper, S. (2002). Post-intellectuality? Universities and the knowledge economy. In S. Cooper, J. Hinkson, & G. Sharp (eds.), *Scholars and entrepreneurs: The universities in crisis* (pp. 207–232). North Carlton, Victoria: Arena Publications.

Derrida, J. (1995). *The gift of death*, trans. D. Wills. Chicago and London: University of Chicago Press.

Drucker, P.F. (1993). *Post-capitalist society*. Oxford: Butterworth Heinemann.

European Commission (2002). *The sixth framework 2002–2006: Towards a European research area*. Luxembourg: Office for Official Publications of the European Communities.

Freeman, C. & Perez, C. (1988). Structural crises of adjustment, business cycles and investment behaviour. In L. Soete (ed.), *Technical change and economic theory* (pp. 38–66). London: Pinter.

Gaita, R. (2002). The university: Is it finished? In S. Cooper, J. Hinkson, & G. Sharp (eds.), *Scholars and entrepreneurs: The universities in crisis* (pp. 91–108). North Carlton, Victoria: Arena Publications.

———. (2003). Profile: Raymond Gaita. *Symposium: Newsletter of the Australian Academy of the Humanities*, 24 (June), 12–19.

Harvey, D. (1989). *The condition of postmodernity: An enquiry into the origins of cultural change*. Oxford: Blackwell.

Heinzelman, K. (1980). *The economics of the imagination*. Amherst: University of Manchester Press.

Hunter, I. (1992). Aesthetics and cultural studies. In L. Grossberg, C. Nelson, & P. Treichler (eds.), *Cultural studies* (pp. 347–367). London: Routledge.

Jameson, F. (1991). *Postmodernism, or the cultural logic of late capitalism*. London: Verso.

Lyotard, J.-F. (1984). *The postmodern condition: A report on knowledge*, trans. G. Bennington & B. Massumi. Minneapolis: University of Minnesota Press.

———. (1993). *Libidinal economy*, trans. I. Hamilton Grant. London: Athlone (first published in 1974 as *Économie libidinale*).

Mauss, M. (1967). *The gift: Forms and functions of exchange in archaic societies*, trans. I. Cunnison. New York: Norton (first published 1925).

Nelson, R.R. & Winter, S. (1982). *An evolutionary theory of economic change*. Cambridge, MA: Harvard University Press.

OECD (Organization for Economic Cooperation and Development) (1996). *The knowledge-based economy*. Paris: OECD.

Osteen, M. & Woodmansee, M. (1999). Taking account of the new economic criticism: An historical introduction. In M. Osteen & M. Woodmansee (eds.), *The new economic criticism: Studies at the intersection of literature and economics* (pp. 3–50). London: Routledge.

Perez, C. (1985). Microelectronics, long waves and world structural system: New perspectives for developing countries. *World Development*, *13*, 441–463.

Romer, P. (1990). Endogenous technological change. *Journal of Political Economy, 98* (5), S71–S102.

———. (1994). The origins of endogenous growth. *Journal of Economic Perspectives, 8,* 3–22.

Ruthven, K. (1998). The future of disciplines: A report on ignorance. In Australian Academy of the Humanities (ed.), *Knowing ourselves and others: The humanities in Australia into the 21st century. Vol. 3, Reflective essays* (pp. 95–112). Canberra: Commonwealth of Australia.

Schumpeter, J.A. (1934). *The theory of economic development: An inquiry into profits, capital, credit interest, and the business cycle.* London: Oxford University Press.

———. (1939). *Business cycles: A theoretical, historical, and statistical analysis of the capitalist process.* New York: McGraw-Hill.

Shell, M. (1982). *Money language and thought: Literary and philosophical economies from the medieval to the modern era.* Berkeley, CA: University of California Press.

## ·2·

*Elizabeth Bullen, Jane Kenway, & Simon Robb*

# CAN THE ARTS AND HUMANITIES SURVIVE THE KNOWLEDGE ECONOMY? A BEGINNER'S GUIDE TO THE ISSUES

We have begun this book with a provocation—a textual irritant designed to problematize the notion of the knowledge economy. Offered as the only viable and virtuous path to disciplinary and university survival, and also to nation building, economic growth, and technological adaptation, knowledge economy policies have taken on characteristics common to all metanarratives—they offer salvation to those who will follow and damnation to those who do not, will not, or cannot. The knowledge economy metanarrative, couched in the hyper-rational language of international governmental bodies and national governments, is powerful and oppressive. Our provocation satirizes this narrative. Its purpose is to take the edge off its power, to make it seem ridiculous by hyper-extending the logic latent within it. We seek to disturb its inexorable rationality, to help to create some space within this narrative for another way of working with notions of "knowledge" and "economy." Our hope is to lift a little of the burden placed on those disciplines that, beneath the weight of current polices, have begun to see themselves as the knowledge economy damned.

The knowledge economy has created a crisis of legitimacy for higher education and research in the arts and humanities. Under conditions of an increasingly competitive global market economy, developed nations and international policy organizations have developed knowledge economy policies that have become a lever of change in higher education teaching and research. These policies (see, for example, OECD, 1996) identify the rise of knowledge-intensive productivity, the globalization of economic activity, and the networked character of economies and cultures as key features of the global knowledge economy (for commentary, see Marginson, 2002; Castells, 2000). Policy responses to this environment, influenced by the same New Growth theories (Cortright, 2001) embraced by the Bush administration in the United States, typically orientate higher education to an innovation system or process that positions knowledge as the key factor of economic growth.

Despite gestures to the arts and humanities such as the United Kingdom's creative industries push and its establishment of an Arts and Humanities Research Board in 1998, the general trend in higher education is towards privileging those knowledge disciplines most amenable to commercialization. Hence, the focus has been on science and technology research and collaboration between universities and industry—see, for example, the European Commission's *Sixth Framework* (2002) and the Commonwealth of Australia's *Backing Australia's Ability* (2001) as well as the various U.K. White Papers (Department of Trade and Industry, 1998, 2000, 2001). One consequence of this trend has been a consistent tension in policy discourse which makes claims about the value of the arts and humanities, but resiles from the apparent incompatibility of these disciplines with the commercial and entrepreneurial orientation of the innovation system (see, for example, World Bank, 2002).

The purpose of this book is to investigate and speculate on some of the ways in which arts and humanities higher education and research can respond in this global policy environment. How the tensions are played out at the level of international and national higher education policy, within university arts and humanities departments, and within the process of writing itself, are the subjects of this book. Its aim is to provide a critical engagement with the key issues as well as conceptual and other resources to assist those in the arts and humanities to think about future directions these disciplines might take. It offers the perspectives of arts and humanities scholars from a range of disciplinary backgrounds including French, philosophy, literary studies, and architecture; the traditional disciplines (history), the new humanities (cultural studies), the creative arts (visual arts) and the creative industries (media studies). The contributors to this volume represent a range of stances toward the key question of whether the arts and humanities should adopt, adapt, or resist knowledge economy policy imperatives. To answer this question, they employ a variety of approaches and strategies, including theory (subcultural theory, poetics, ethics), theorists (Deleuze, Guattari, Derrida, Hunter, Agamben), and modes of inquiry (policy analysis, case study, history, comparative analysis, philosophical meditation, satire).

The subject of this chapter is the knowledge economy itself, and its aim is to map the evolution of the policy terrain which the arts and humanities must now negotiate. It offers an overview of how and why the knowledge economy policies are reshaping knowledge production in the higher education and research environment and some of the implications for the arts and humanities.

### A Short History of the Knowledge Economy

The notion of the knowledge economy made a decisive entry into policy discourses when the Organization for Economic Cooperation and Development (OECD) published *The Knowledge-Based Economy* (1996). This report outlines trends and implications for employment and government; the role of the science system; and indicators of the knowledge-based economy. It defines knowledge-based economies as "economies which are directly based on the production, distribution and use of knowledge and information" (OECD, 1996, p. 7). In this document, the knowledge-based economy functions as the overarching term that encompasses variant and related notions of the information society, network society, and learning economy. These concepts are generally oriented toward and facilitated by information and communications technology in the global economy. However, these terms are also frequently confused with the knowledge economy and each other (Peters, 2001). Indeed, the very existence of the phenomena this family of terms purportedly represents is contested (May, 2002; Webster, 1995).

One of the reasons for this confusion—and contestation—is that the *idea* of what we here call the knowledge economy emerged much earlier than the 1990s. As we show elsewhere (Kenway, Bullen, & Robb, in progress), the genealogy we will sketch in this chapter begins in the late 1950s and, depending on disciplinary and conceptual perspectives and emphases, has seen a range terms used to describe this evolving phenomenon. Beniger (1986, pp. 4–5) lists some 75 terms coined to describe contemporary socioeconomic and technology-driven change between 1950 and 1984 alone.

The seeds of the idea of a knowledge society/economy were sown by Professor of Management Peter Drucker (1959) who coined the terms "knowledge worker," "knowledge work," and "knowledge industries." It was around this time that white-collar workers first outnumbered blue-collar workers in the U.S. workforce (Naisbitt, 1984). Later Machlup (1962) calculated that 29 per cent of the U.S. gross national product (GNP) derived from knowledge industries: education; research and development (R&D); communications media; information machines (i.e. computers); and information services including finance, insurance, and real estate. Drucker (1969) is credited with introducing the concepts of the knowledge economy and knowledge society.

However, others argue that the notion of the knowledge economy had its roots elsewhere in the literature of postindustrialism (see also Masuda, 1980; Touraine, 1974), in particular the version theorized by sociologist Daniel Bell (1976). Bell anticipated a number of the key features of the knowledge economy including the centrality of the computer and ICTs, the construction of knowledge as a commodity, and the replacement of labor and capital with information and knowledge. He uses the terms "knowledge society" (1976) and "information society" (1976, 1979), but rejects both in favor of "postindustrial society." Later he was to relent on this, conceding that a new social framework based on information technology and telecommunications "may be decisive for the way economic and social exchanges are conducted, the way knowledge is created and retrieved, and the character of work and occupations in which men [*sic*] are engaged" (Bell, 1979, p. 533).

Indeed, driven by the advances in and diffusion of information and communication technologies (ICTs), the so-called information revolution saw "knowledge" displaced by "information" as the source of economic growth (Porat, 1977). The currency of the information society and information economy during the 1970s and 1980s may have been assisted by hype surrounding technological change and the rapid spread of information networks. Certainly, information technologies were privileged over other forms of technology as a factor of economic growth. Information, unlike knowledge, can be encoded and distributed via ICTs, and it is therefore more easily quantified, even if the quantification of information remains contentious (Roszak, 1986; Webster 1995). By the end of the 1970s, a number of national governments including Japan (Ministry of International Trade and Industry, 1969), France (Nora & Minc, 1978), and Canada (Valaskakis, 1979) had developed explicit information society policies.

Yet, as Morris-Suzuki (1988, p. 8) points out, "the term 'information society' is one which is more often used than defined." Although its "comfortable elasticity of definition" does not mean that "the concept is a vacuous one" (Morris-Suzuki, 1988, p. 8), it is perhaps this lack of precision that saw the emergence of competing terms in the 1990s. Theories of the learning society and learning economy appeared in the early 1990s and, as indicated above, "knowledge economy" and "knowledge society" re-appeared in the mid-1990s. Their use has been equally imprecise, although it is arguable that each represents an inflection of a fundamental idea. This is evident in, for example, the way in which "knowledge society" is defined in policies (when it is defined at all). Knowledge society is evidently a broader and more inclusive concept than knowledge economy. However, while it may encompass the social distribution of knowledge and is frequently used in policy in regard to employment and education, the basic definition of the knowledge society in policy documents remains remarkably similar to those of the knowledge economy (see, for example, European Commission, 2003, p. 2).

One reason for this slippage—and our preference for the term knowledge economy—is that, although the conceptual tributaries to the knowledge economy debates are many and growing (management, sociology, policy studies, futurology, politics, education, cultural studies—and in this volume, the arts and humanities), it is economics that has been the most influential in policy conceptualizations. It is notable that sociological explorations, with their more comprehensive analyses of the social benefits and risks of politico-economic change, are rarely referred to in policies.

Still, while the knowledge economy is related to the information society, it is not simply the information society under a different brand. It reappears in policy discourses as part of an evolving conceptual trajectory. Knowledge is a far broader concept than information, which ultimately comes down to data. Likewise, technology in the knowledge economy includes, but goes well beyond, information technologies. Indeed, it is not a particular technology *per se* that drives the economy, although some neo-Schumpeterian economists link dominant technologies with economic cycles (Perez, 1983, 1985) and elsewhere we have examined the influence of this techno-economic paradigm (Bullen, Robb, & Kenway, 2004; Robb & Bullen, this volume). According to New Growth (Romer, 1986) and other influential endogenous growth theories (Howitt, 2000), economic growth is driven by technological progress or innovation that involves the inputs of existing knowledge and human capital to make new and improved knowledge products. Technological change is oriented to market imperatives and is equated with knowledge generated through applied or commercial research (OECD, 1996). Indeed, it is "the context of application" that "describes the total environment in which scientific problems arise, methodologies are developed, outcomes are disseminated and uses are defined" (Nowotny, Scott, & Gibbons, forthcoming).

Endogenous growth theory differs from classical economic theory, which acknowledges the importance of knowledge to economic growth but regards knowledge as exogenous—that is external to—the economic process or growth model (Solow, 1970). In endogenous models of macro-economic growth, the knowledge is endogenous, that is, internal, to the model, and grows as a result of maximizing the behavior of knowledge workers and knowledge resources.

It is this that puts higher education and research at the center of economic policies and that makes investment in human capital via education and training and funding of research and development so important to economic growth. It is this that helps us better understand the significance of policy intervention in higher education and research, and funding incentives for the development of, for example:

- research "clusters" and "centers of excellence" to assist with the generation of new knowledge and critical mass;
- transdisciplinary and transnational networks to assist with access to the best knowledge;
- collaborative relationships with firms to help spread risk and resources and to assist with the commercialization of research; and
- a new generation of researchers adept in the so-called "enabling" sciences (mathematics, physics, and chemistry) which will service the biotechnology, nanotechnology, information technology, and as yet unimagined industries.

All of these measures are designed to maximize knowledge production and thus economic growth.

The effect of this on the research environment has been profound, not least in regard to knowledge production itself. The concepts of Mode 1 and Mode 2 knowledge production theorized by Gibbons, Limoges, Nowotny, Schwartzman, Scott, and Trow (1994) provide one account of this change (see also Jeffcutt; Redshaw, this volume). In *The New Production of Knowledge: The Dynamics of Science and Research in Contemporary Societies*, the authors distinguish between the cognitive and social practices of Mode 1 (or traditional, specialized academic) knowledge which is exogenous, and Mode 2 (or socially distributed) knowledge which is endogenous to the innovation process. Elsewhere, Gibbons (1994, online) summarizes further differences between the two:

> in Mode 1 problems are set and solved in a context governed by the, largely academic, interests of a specific community. By contrast, Mode 2 knowledge is carried out in a context of application. Mode 1 is disciplinary while Mode 2 is transdisciplinary. Mode 1 is characterized by homogeneity, Mode 2 by heterogeneity. Organizationally, Mode 1 is hierarchical and tends to preserve its form, while Mode 2 is heterarchical and transient. Each employs a different type of quality control. In comparison with Mode 1, Mode 2 is more socially accountable and reflexive. It includes a wider, more temporary and heterogeneous set of practitioners, collaborating on a problem defined in a specific and localized context.

The shift to issue-based, collaborative, and transdisciplinary research with commercial applications may have initially represented an adaptation or accommodation to the evolving knowledge economy—in particular, the massification of higher education and competition for resources in the post-welfare state (see Macintyre, this volume). However, taken up by policy makers (for example, Kemp, 1999; OECD, 1996), the notion of Mode 2 knowledge production has become increasingly prescriptive, even if this is currently a matter of favor (funding) rather than penalty.

Nowotny, Scott, and Gibbons (forthcoming) acknowledge the way in which their thesis has been exploited, oversimplified, and opportunistically manipulated by academics and policy makers alike. Their original 1994 thesis is much broader than the focus on Mode 2 knowledge production would imply. Reflecting on the five contexts in which Mode 2 knowledge developed, Nowotny et al. (forthcoming) describe the role of the humanities in knowledge production. They say the humanities are

> the most engaged of all disciplines, not simply because they flow through the culture industry (for example, through novels or popular history) but because they comfortably and inevitably embody notions of reflexivity which the natural, and even the social, sciences distrust normatively and methodologically.

The authors now argue that it is necessary to think beyond the context of "application" as the total environment of knowledge production, which they say actually reinforces hierarchical, linear, and positivist approaches. They suggest that what is needed is a capacity "to reach beyond the knowable context of application to the unknowable context of implication" (Nowotny et al., forthcoming). This involves reflexivity and reflexivity is an expertise that the humanities are well placed to provide (see also Bullen, Robb, & Kenway, 2004).

Unfortunately, in the clamor to become competitive knowledge economies, too many advanced economies are continuing to prioritize applied research and entrepreneurial activities, with clear and often short-term commercial pay-offs; to dictate research priorities (Cunningham; Macintyre, this volume); to privilege corporate values over academic values in decision making (Anyanwu, this volume); and to evaluate research performance in ways that create particular problems—and opportunities—for the arts and humanities.

## Adopt, Adapt, Resist?

The knowledge economy and associated policies place new pressures on the arts and humanities and raise questions about their role. The techno-economic orientation of policy impacts on what research is supported or promoted, and traditional arts and humanities faculties fare poorly under this new rubric. Current knowledge economy policies intensify the already pervasive view of a dichotomy between learning for its own sake and learning that is instrumental (see Robb & Bullen, this volume). Despite the commercial success of the creative industries and the British initiatives indicated above (Jeffcutt, this volume), many policies fail to pay much more than lip service to the social, cultural, intellectual, and, indeed, economic role of the humanities (Cunningham, this volume). The viability of research in the humanities is further compromised by the economic rationalization to which many disciplines are increasingly subject.

It is our view that the fundamental value of higher education teaching and research in the arts and humanities is not in question. The benefits of such scholarship (Bigelow, 1998, p. 37) include:

- the vital role it plays in intellectual freedom;
- the indispensable service it provides through critical analysis;
- the provision of a sense of place in history and the world;
- its function as a key player in public culture;
- the preservation and transmission of traditions from one generation to the next;
- the questioning and maintenance of ethical values; and
- thinking constructively about what the future may hold.

However, as we have argued elsewhere (Bullen, Robb, & Kenway, 2004), these qualities are also largely intangible, certainly not technology-driven, and problematic in terms of producing measurable economic outcomes. Linked to national benefit, they may indeed contribute to informed policy making, social cohesion, and provide employer-friendly skills such as those identified by the Royal Society of Arts as "communicating effectively, teamwork, negotiation, co-operation" (Bayliss, 1999, p. 15). These are skills that have been identified in a range of policies (see for example CERI, 2001) as the generic skills of the knowledge worker, but they are difficult to measure quantitatively. Ironically, they are probably easier to quantify than the other competencies and values that arts and humanities scholarship impart.

Faculties of the arts and humanities feel increasingly compelled to justify their existence within the techno-economic understandings of the knowledge economy via the rhetoric of technologization and commercialization, innovation, and collaboration. Foregrounding the imperative to commercialize, Gillies (2001, p. 42) iterates some of the particular difficulties commercialization poses for the humanities and social sciences in terms of researcher autonomy and research for the public good, but concludes that these disciplines "risk deeper penury and even depiction as the Luddites of the twenty-first century, unless they can embrace the commercializing spirit." This view captures the deep ambivalence many feel in the current environment, but it is also a view that is ultimately reductive and insufficiently reflexive. To paraphrase Nowotny et al. (forthcoming), it fails to do what they suggest the humanities are best placed to do, and that is to address "the unknowable context of implication," in this case, the implication of our own responses to the current crisis (see also Loo, this volume).

Our ability to critically interrogate our own position—and the challenge to the legitimacy of the arts and humanities in the knowledge economy policy environment—is too often limited by binary thinking: public versus market interests, science versus humanities, tradition versus innovation, vocational versus liberal education, basic versus applied research, aesthetic versus cognitive. At the same time, the exigencies of academic life are such that too many in the arts and humanities are only able to experience the impact of knowledge economy policies at a system level, with little opportunity to reflect upon the broader contexts and implications of this global phenomenon. Among those who do, there is little consensus as to whether to adapt, adopt, or resist the new policy imperatives.

The purpose of this book is to represent some of these various and often conflicting stances and to explore ways in which the arts and humanities might practically and innovatively reconstruct themselves under knowledge economy policies. It seeks to do this in a number of ways.

First, it seeks to locate the challenges facing the arts and humanities in the context of the global policy environment, international trends in higher education and research, and at a national and system level. Kenway, Bullen, & Robb situate the development of knowledge economy policies within the broader context of globalization. They focus on the increasingly influential role of supranational organizations such as the OECD, World Bank, and UNESCO in higher education and research policy. Cunningham examines the way in which standard innovation and research and development agendas are evolving internationally, and the problems with them. Taking the example of the creative industries, he makes the case for including the humanities and creative arts in these agendas. Macintyre, meanwhile, explores the impact of knowledge economy policies in the context of the history of higher education teaching and research in the humanities in Australia to provide a case study and a context for an analysis of their impact in other countries.

Second, this book seeks to explore ways in which the policy debate might be challenged or critically reinterpreted from a theoretical perspective and through aesthetic means. Given that debates about the role and value of the arts and humanities are largely circumscribed by policy contexts, it is perhaps not surprising that the theoretical, critical, and aesthetic resources of arts and humanities are rarely utilized in their defense. However, in tailoring arguments to the policy context, there is a risk of forfeiting some of the intellectual rigor that is needed to think about the issues as scholars. Those in the arts and humanities must draw on these resources if they are to be able to think critically and decisively about whether and how to adopt, adapt, and resist the knowledge economy. Hainge argues that philosophy itself can be affirmed not merely as a discipline but a basic, inherent principle of the university. Drawing on Derrida's notion of forgiveness, Hainge argues that the very conditions of possibility for philosophy, within a techno-economic paradigm, would today seem to depend on its ability to navigate between two poles, one abstract and seemingly universal, the other pragmatic and situated. Further, drawing on Deleuze's work on immanence, Hainge argues that the mode of pragmatic governance of any system is inherent and immanent to it and that to impose an external, knowledge economy governance will simply result in the production of intellectual "waste" and "noise." In his chapter, Loo presents a philosophical inquiry into the ethico-aesthetic "obligation" of the arts and humanities to accommodate technological and economic imperatives. With reference to Deleuze, Guattari, and Agamben, and taking the work of Dutch architect Koolhass, he argues that it is possible for the arts and humanities to do their ethical and aesthetic work within a techno-economic paradigm. Walker's chapter is an example of this idea. It enacts research as writing, performing an encounter with the difficult textual surface that the arts and humanities run into. In so doing it considers the art of Patricia Piccinini, who works on/with the space between aesthetics and science. Walker's chapter is both a type of writing as research and a discussion of an aesthetic practice that produces a surface on which we can trace the contours of the ethical and epistemological concerns opening out in the knowledge economy.

Third, this book investigates ways in which the arts and humanities can constructively adapt without compromise to knowledge economy imperatives. Anyanwu explores the benefits of transdisciplinary knowledge production. He takes the example of an interdisciplinary research group to argue that the humanities need not be the handmaid of science and technology, and the example of a media studies program to show that, rather than threatening the future of disciplinary knowledge, collaboration with industry partners in education can help achieve the critical mass to preserve it. Likewise, it is Redshaw's case that collaboration with industry should not be understood only in terms of commercialization. She suggests that, in terms of knowledge production, collaboration has the potential to contribute more to the public good than liberal education and uses a successful research project on the cultures of driving to make her case.

Fourth, this book seeks to show how a theoretical critique that problematizes key knowledge economy concepts can be combined with an innovative community engagement and socially produced knowledge. To counter the reductive nature of the knowledge economy, Potter draws on Deleuze and Guattari to propose a "knowledge ecology" and brings this to bear on the work of artist and spatial historian Paul Carter. Luckman challenges the conceptualization of innovation with reference to youth subcultural theory.

Finally, and crucially, this book makes the case that successful positioning of the arts and humanities within the knowledge economy is a task of the research endeavor itself. Concentrating on the creative industries, Jeffcutt explores the problems and opportunities created within the complex field concerned with creativity in knowledge economies and focuses on the dynamics of connectivity.

## References

Bayliss, V. (1999). *Opening minds: Education for the 21st century*. London: Royal Society of Arts.

Bell, D. (1976). *The coming of post-industrial society: A venture in social forecasting*. New York: Basic Books (first published 1973).

———. (1979). The social framework of the information society. In M.L. Dertouzos & J. Moses (eds.), *The computer age: A twenty-year view* (pp. 500–549). Cambridge, MA: MIT Press.

Beniger, J.R. (1986). *The control revolution: Technological and economic origins of the information society*. Cambridge, MA: Harvard University Press.

Bigelow, J. (1998). Valuing humanities research. In Australian Academy of the Humanities (ed.), *Knowing ourselves and others: The humanities in Australia into the 21st century, Volume 3, Reflective essays* (pp. 37–58). Canberra: Commonwealth of Australia.

Bullen, E., Robb, S., & Kenway, J. (2004). "Creative destruction": Knowledge economy policy and the future of the arts and humanities in the academy. *Journal of Education Policy, 19* (1), 3–22.

Castells, M. (2000). *The rise of the network society*. Oxford: Blackwell.

CERI (Centre for Educational Research and Innovation) (2001). *Education policy analysis 2001*. Paris: OECD Publications, available online http://www.suc.unam.mx/riseu/documentos/epa2001.pdf

Commonwealth of Australia (2001). *Backing Australia's ability: An innovation action plan for the future*. Canberra: Commonwealth of Australia.

Cortright, J. (2001). New growth theory, technology and learning: A practitioners' guide. *Reviews of Economic Development Literature and Practice, 4*, available online http://www.impresaconsulting.com/cortright_ngt.pdf

Creative Industries, Queensland University of Technology (Website) http://www.creativeindustries.qut.com/courses/course-major.jsp?major-id=1213

Centre for Creative Industry, Queen's University, Belfast (Website) http://www.creative.qub.ac.uk/

Department of Trade and Industry (U.K.) (1998). *Our competitive future: Building the knowledge-driven economy.* London: DTI, available online http://www.dti.gov.uk/comp/competitive/main.htm

———. (2000). *Excellence and opportunity: A science and innovation policy for the 21st century.* CM 4814. London: DTI, available online http://www.ost.gov.uk/enterprise/excellence.htm

———. (2001). *Opportunity for all in a world of change.* CM 5042. London: DTI, available online http://www.dti.gov.uk/opportunityforall/index.html

Drucker, P.F. (1959). *Landmarks of tomorrow.* New York: Harper.

———. (1969). *The age of discontinuity: Guidelines to our changing society.* New York: Harper and Row.

European Commission (2002). *Participating in European research: Sixth framework programme (2002–2006).* Luxembourg: Office for Official Publications of the European Communities.

———. (2003). *The role of universities in the Europe of knowledge.* COM(2003)58 final, 5 February. Brussels: European Commission, available online http://europa.eu.int/comm/education/doc/official/keydoc/2003/univ_en.pdf

Gibbons, M. (1994, August). *Innovation and the developing system of knowledge production.* Paper presented at Innovation, Competitiveness and Sustainability in the North American Region, Simon Fraser University, British Columbia, Canada, available online http://edie.cprost.sfu.ca/summer/papers/Michael.Gibbons.html

Gibbons, M., Limoges, C., Nowotny, H., Schwartzman, S., Scott, P., & Trow, M. (1994). *The new production of knowledge: The dynamics of science and research in contemporary societies.* London: Sage.

Gillies, M. (2001). Commercialization and globalization. In Department of Education, Training and Youth Affairs (ed.), *National Humanities and Social Sciences Summit, 2001, Position papers* (pp. 41–48). Canberra: Commonwealth of Australia.

Howitt, P. (2000). Endogenous growth and cross-country income differences. *American Economic Review, 90,* 829–846.

Kemp, D. (1999). *New knowledge, new opportunities: A discussion paper on higher education research and research training.* Canberra: Commonwealth of Australia, available online *http://www.dest.gov.au/archive/highered/otherpub/greenpaper/contents.htm*

Kenway, J., Bullen, E., & Robb, S. (in progress). *Haunting the knowledge economy.*

Machlup, F. (1962). *The production and distribution of knowledge in the United States.* Princeton, NJ: Princeton University Press.

Marginson, S. (2002). *What's wrong with the universities?* Melbourne: Arena.

Masuda, Y. (1980). *The information society as post-industrial society.* Washington, DC: World Futures Society.

May, C. (2002). *The information society: A sceptical view.* Cambridge: Polity Press.

Ministry of International Trade and Industry (1969). *Toward the information society: Report of the Industrial Structure Council.* Tokyo: Computer Age.

Morris-Suzuki, T. (1988). *Beyond computopia: Information, automation and democracy in Japan.* London: Kegan Paul.

Naisbitt, J. (1984). *Megatrends: Ten new directions transforming our lives.* London: MacDonald.

Nora, S. & Minc, A. (1978). *L'informatisation de la société.* Paris: La Documentation Francaise.

Nowotny, H., Scott, P., & Gibbons, M. (forthcoming). Re-thinking science: Mode 2 in societal context. In *Technology, innovation and knowledge: Management book series, Vol. 2: Knowledge creation, diffusion and use in innovation networks and clusters: A comparative systems approach across the US, Europe and Asia.* Westport, CT: Greenwood Publishing Group Praeger Books, available online http://www.nowotny.ethz.ch/pdf/Nowotny_Gibbons_Scott_Mode2.pdf

OECD (Organization for Economic Cooperation and Development) (1996). *The knowledge-based economy.* Paris: OECD.

Perez, C. (1985). Microelectronics, long waves and world structural system: New perspectives for developing countries. *World Development, 13,* 441–463.

———. (1983). Structural change and the assimilation of new technologies in the economic and social system. *Futures, 15,* 357–375.

Peters, M. (2001). National education policy constructions of the "knowledge economy": towards a critique. *Journal of Educational Enquiry, 2* (1), 1–22.

Porat, M.U. (1977). The information economy: Definition and measurement. *The Information Economy, 1,* 22–29.

Romer, P. (1986). Increasing returns and long run growth. *Journal of Political Economy, 94* (5), 1002–1037.

Roszak, T. (1986). *The cult of information: The folklore of computers and the true art of thinking.* New York: Pantheon Books.

Solow, R. (1970). *Growth theory: An exposition.* Oxford: Clarendon Press.

Touraine, A. (1974). *The post-industrial society: Tomorrow's social history: Classes, conflicts and culture in programmed society.* New York: Wildwood House.

Valaskakis, K. (1979). *The information society: The issues and the choices. Integrating report for the Information Society Project.* Ottawa: Department of Communications.

Webster, F. (1995). *Theories of the information society.* New York: Routledge.

World Bank (2002). *Constructing knowledge societies: New challenges for tertiary education.* Washington, DC: World Bank, available online http://www1.worldbank.org/education/pdf/Constructing%20Knowledge%20Societies.pdf

# · 3 ·

*Stuart Macintyre*

---

# THE HUMANITIES IN THE KNOWLEDGE ECONOMY

The notion of a link between economic growth and higher education and research is not new, but it arguably crystallized in the knowledge economy policies and related New Growth economic theory that emerged in the 1990s. As this chapter will show, universities have been shaped over time in response to external social, cultural, and economic pressures and, as others in this volume explain, by internal crises such as debates over liberal education (Redshaw) and the new humanities (Cunningham). Bauman (1997) argues that the current challenges confronting universities have been intensified by *change in the way change occurs*—what he calls "meta-change." The world for which universities evolved was more stable. It took time for

> skills to become obsolete, for specialisms to be relabelled as blinkers, for bold heresies to turn into retrograde orthodoxies, and all in all for the assets to turn into liabilities. Such a world . . . is now vanishing and the sheer speed of vanishing is much in excess of the readjustment and redeployment capacity the universities have acquired over the centuries. (Bauman, 1997, p. 24)

Under these circumstances, Bauman suggests, our habitual responses to change or crisis may have dire consequences

The rapidity of change to which Bauman refers has been accelerated by globalization and technological advances in information and communications technologies. They have worked together to alter flows in both time and space, assisting the dissemination of knowledge economy policy globally as well as international flows of students, staff, and educational services. One outcome of this is a convergence in the higher education and research policy thinking of different countries. Global and international policy development is becoming more relevant to policy development at a local or national level. So, too, is an understanding of the university systems to which researchers in other countries belong, and with whom we are increasingly encouraged to network and collaborate.

Alan Wagner, the tertiary education policy specialist and author of *Redefining Tertiary Education* (1998), identifies three policy tendencies in higher education and research (Wagner, 2003, p. 54). They are: *broad-based*, and relate to investment in and development of human capital; *innovative*, and relate to performance-based funding, tuition fees, standards, and governance; and exhibit *sustained policy attention* to higher education reform. Wagner identifies these trends to varying degrees in a range of OECD countries including Australia, Denmark, Germany, Ireland, Japan, the Netherlands, New Zealand, Norway, the United Kingdom, and the United States. He also argues that higher education policy makers and education leaders would benefit from closer scrutiny of "the accumulating policy experience in other countries" (Wagner, 2003, p. 55).

The impact of these changes is perhaps felt no more acutely or with as much ambivalence as by the humanities, those disciplines that are concerned with understanding and appreciation of human creativity, together with reflection and critical inquiry on the abiding concerns of humanity.[1] This chapter explores some of the key problems these disciplines face and how these have evolved in regard to the pressures of the knowledge economy. To do this, it charts a historical trajectory of higher education teaching and research in the humanities in Australia to provide a case study and a context for an analysis of the impact of equivalent knowledge economy policies in other countries.

### *The Evolution of the Humanities in Australia*

Australian universities began as outposts of a received cultural tradition. The purpose of the nineteenth-century civic universities of Sydney, Melbourne, and Adelaide was to civilize colonial Australians with a curriculum taken from British universities and based on classics, philosophy, and mathematics (Gardner, 1979). Since that activity attracted too few adherents, they made themselves useful by training the learned professions. These universities were teaching institutions, passing on received bodies of knowledge. They were places of privilege, accessible only to a select few, and largely remote from public life (Macintyre & Marginson, 1999).

It was in the sciences that the idea of the advancement of knowledge through research first took root. The research ethos—the pursuit of knowledge as its own end—was assisted by the application of knowledge to national purposes. Two world wars led to calls for an enhanced scientific capacity. The needs of industry required increasing technical expertise, while an advanced industrial society required additional expertise in administration and social policy. These were the arguments that persuaded Australia's state governments to establish faculties of engineering, agricultural and veterinary science, economics, and commerce, and the federal government to embark on a major expansion after it assumed responsibility for higher education in the 1950s.

The postwar expansion of higher education encompassed economics, psychology, sociology, and other social sciences because of their contribution to national tasks. This trend towards disciplinary specialization was intensified by the demand of government and industry for greater professional expertise, and it eroded the unitary idea of the university (Smith & Webster, 1997). Nevertheless, the inquiry conducted by the Murray Committee in 1957 insisted that Australian universities must provide "a full and true education" in the humanities for "rounded human beings" (Poynter & Rasmussen, 1996, pp. 181–183). Such a viewpoint affirmed the notion of a liberal education and its core values, which include the cultivation of character and citizenship (see Redshaw, this volume). It was assumed that all disciplines should ground their teaching in research. The social sciences and the humanities followed the natural sciences in the expectation that learning must follow the advance of knowledge.

In such circumstances the humanities and social sciences came rapidly to life. Large departments were assembled and postgraduate research degrees established; the first doctorate of philosophy in Australia was awarded in 1948. Professional associations were formed, journals and academic presses created. Libraries built collections capable of supporting research, which was supported with study leave and grants to support overseas travel. Australian scholars began to make a sustained contribution to their disciplines, to participate more fully in international activities and to gain international recognition of their contributions.

This enhanced capacity provided Australians with an augmented understanding of the rest of the world and their place within it. The Research School of Pacific Studies at the Australian National University became a principal site of work on the island societies to our north and east. Through studies of Asian languages, and the history, politics, economies, and culture of South-East and East Asian countries, Australians reoriented their bearing on the region they had formerly known as the Far East (Asian Studies Association, 2002).

The contribution of the humanities and social sciences to national life in the second half of the twentieth century was profound. Educational research informed the changing school curriculum; urban studies improved the cities. Demographers and sociologists guided the acceptance of ethnic diversity; scholars of literature, art, and music helped us to read, see, and hear Australian work; lexicographers assisted us to appreciate its distinctive speech; historians enabled recognition of a binding past. The causes that animate us—human rights, the green movement, feminism—all draw on the work of scholarship in the humanities (Australian Research Council, 1998a, 1998b). Economists developed the levers for steering the economy through the expansive years of full employment, and then led the turn back to the market.

This flourishing of the humanities coincided with developments in communication technologies, microelectronics, computing, biotechnology, and robotics which would contribute to the third industrial revolution, variously called post-industrial, knowledge, or information society among many other titles, and which in this volume we call the knowledge economy. The basis of this revolution was not machine technology or the production of tangible goods or services, but the production and dissemination of information and knowledge (Jones, 1995). As Kenway, Bullen, and Robb (in progress) describe, the effect of this was soon felt in universities. They point to Kerr (1963, pp. 87–88), who argued that the "growth of the 'knowledge industry,' which is coming to permeate government and business and to draw into it more and more people raised to higher and higher levels of skill," was already changing the character of universities. He identified these changes, which we see intensified today, as the education of unprecedented numbers of students, industry collaboration, the adaptation of new intellectual currents, and entrepreneurialism.

These trends were intensified in the mid-1970s as a consequence of the OPEC oil crisis and subsequent world recession. Although this economic downturn was arguably a by-product of the transition to a post-industrial society (Jones, 1995), it was also a key impetus for the formation of information society policy, a precursor of the knowledge economy (Kenway, Bullen, & Robb, in progress). In Australia, the combination of a faltering economy and an increased demand for higher education placed the university system under increasing strain. When John Dawkins, then federal Minister for Education in the incumbent Australian Labor government, reformed the sector in the mid-1980s, he aligned it to the government's goals. Research was explicitly oriented to the national economy, higher education and training to the needs of its workforce. The partial reintroduction of fees through the Higher Education Contribution Scheme was accompanied by a much stronger emphasis on employment outcomes. The opening up of full-fee courses, first for postgraduate coursework degrees and then for international and domestic students, created much stronger vocational pressures (Marginson & Considine, 2000).

Arts students no longer made up the largest group of undergraduates, surpassed by those in business studies. With fewer destinations clearly signposted for arts graduates, the demand from school leavers for a place in arts languished, and many universities responded by cannibalizing their arts degree into more specialized and vocational degrees. These changes, moreover, occurred at a time when careers were becoming increasingly transient and the ability to adapt more important than ever (Pascoe, Ainley, Macintyre, & Williamson, 2003).

The humanities and social sciences currently make up a little less than a fifth of Australian university staff, with another fifth in applied fields such as education and business studies. More of those in the first category are shifting into vocational studies such as tourism, sport, journalism, and public policy. There are few vacancies in language departments, in classics, literature, history, and philosophy, where those who retire are less likely to be replaced.

Higher education reforms in Australia in the 1980s also weakened the link between teaching and research. Some of the public funding that had been provided to the universities to support their research activity was sequestered into a national pool and reallocated to individual researchers and research groups. While peer assessment guided this concentration of research support, the distribution of funds was overlaid by centrally determined priorities and encouragement of industry partnerships.

These changes in research policy strained the humanities, but they have since been overtaken by the extension of the same principles to the core funding of universities. In 1999 the Commonwealth changed its formula for the operating grants of universities. The research component is now determined by measures of performance based primarily on inputs, so that those institutions that attract substantial research income are rewarded. There is a minor and very approximate output factor, publications, which uses definitions and weighting that disadvantage the humanities. Postgraduate research places are now allocated according to similar measures, with stringent requirements for timely completion. Furthermore, a weighting applies that is meant to allow for the differences in the cost of research in different disciplines: the laboratory disciplines receive more than twice as much per candidature as the non-laboratory disciplines. Similar ratios are built in to the system of performance-based research funding that was adopted by the New Zealand higher education sector, and are pervasive in the allocation of public funds to university research.

As universities seek to maximize their share of the available funds, they apply similar formulae to their own funding models. Research support and postgraduate places go to those faculties, departments, centers, and teams that best conform to the Commonwealth's model. The universities are required to formulate research plans that show how they will promote such concentrations of research activity. The growing differentiation of research opportunities has been formalized in the new concept of the "research active staff" (defined on the basis of publication, postgraduate supervision, and research grants). There is a very real danger of recreating the binary divide that Dawkins abolished within the so-called unified system of higher education, a reform paralleled in the United Kingdom with the absorption of the polytechnics into the university system in 1992.

The current Australian federal Liberal government came late to the appreciation of research and innovation as a driver of the knowledge economy. When it did, the Prime Minister's Science, Engineering and Innovation Council played a vital role in the formulation of research policy. A casual observer could be forgiven for thinking that in Canberra the knowledge economy is a shorthand term for developments in the biological and information sciences. Dazzled by the stock exchange boom in the pharmaceuticals and information and communication technology sectors in the late 1990s, inundated by media coverage of breakthroughs in genetics and stem cells, the Commonwealth designated areas of scientific research that were to receive a third of the Australian Research Council's research funding. The Commonwealth's key innovation statement, *Backing Australia's Ability* (2001), explicitly harnessed higher education and research to economic goals.

### Arts and Humanities in the Knowledge Economy

As knowledge economies seek to strengthen their economic competitiveness in the global market, they are taking policy measures to consolidate their research or knowledge base. The European Commission's Framework programs represent the European Community's main strategy for the creation of an integrated European Research Area. The current Sixth Framework Program seeks to strengthen the scientific and technological bases of industry with the aim of making the European Union the most competitive and dynamic knowledge-based economy in the world by 2010. The seven European research priorities, with the exception of "citizens and governance in a knowledge-based society," are science and technology-oriented. The Australian national research priorities, which apply to the national research agencies, are

- an environmentally sustainable Australia
- promoting and maintaining good health
- frontier technologies
- safeguarding Australia

These are by no means the obvious areas in which to concentrate research, but each one of these lends itself to contributions from the humanities and social sciences. However, they were defined and elaborated in a remarkably restrictive manner to exclude much of the work that would fill them out. Safeguarding Australia, for example, turned out to mean protection of information systems through electronic security and prevention of terrorism through voice recognition technology (see also Cunningham, this volume).

As this suggests, the core disciplines of the humanities and social sciences are especially disadvantaged by the combined emphasis on the prioritization of science and technology and on research income as a determinant of funding. They find it difficult to attract industry funding, which is concentrated in the biological and technological sciences. Some of the disciplines are especially disadvantaged by the new conditions on postgraduate research: in linguistics or anthropology, for instance, where substantial fieldwork is required, a candidate will have great difficulty in completing his or her thesis in the time that is required for funding purposes. More generally, the application of simple aggregate measures across the range of research fields pays little heed to issues of quality. For all of its vexations, the British system, where discipline panels evaluate research performance on a qualitative basis, seems to me to be far more conducive to breadth and excellence.

More recently still, scrutiny of the Institutional Grants Scheme, the Research Infrastructure Block Grants, and the Research Training Scheme was announced during the presentation of the 2003 federal budget. The present research performance indicators will be examined and there seems a strong possibility that the present publications count will be abandoned. This is the first of the Australian Research Council's reviews of its six discipline clusters, and it is designed to provide appropriate measures of research in areas that lack the quantitative measures of the sciences. They have well-established procedures for measuring the volume and impact of research through their principal medium, the journal article, but a great deal of research in the humanities occurs in books, electronic media, and other modes that are not captured in citation counts. The review is designed to provide alternative measures through data compiled by the Public and Educational Lending Right Agency, the Copyright Agency Limited, and even media monitors so that we can begin to understand the ways in which work in the humanities circulates. There is also to be a study of concentrations in research centers and institutes, and a survey of leading national and international researchers to identify national strengths.

A parallel process is currently underway in the United States, where the American Academy of the Arts and Sciences is conducting a project on statistical indicators for the humanities as part of its Initiative for Humanities and Culture. The Humanities Indicators are modeled on the U.S. National Science Foundation's Science and Engineering Indicators, and "will eventually provide much-needed information about the humanities workforce, the importance of humanities studies to American education and civic life, and the future of humanities education" (American Academy of the Arts and Sciences, online). The British Academy (online) is likewise engaged in a study that will seek to quantify and provide firm evidence of the contributions of the humanities and social sciences to "the knowledge-driven economy."

### *What Does This Mean for Research in the Humanities?*

An answer to this question will be assisted when these processes are completed. In the absence of such data, my observations are necessarily tentative. I can, however, draw on my insight as a member of the Australian Research Council panel, which, I first emphasize, maintains a strong commitment to supporting research across the full range of its disciplines, including the traditional humanities disciplines.

However, there is a noticeable trend toward collaborative and interdisciplinary research prescribed by knowledge economy policy. Just as it is common in scientific research to assemble a team with different forms of expertise to contribute to the pursuit of a particular objective, so it is becoming more common to find scholars in history or literature working on a project with the assistance of expertise in multimedia or cultural policy. Researchers in the humanities have proved to be adept in establishing partnerships with public, voluntary, and private sector stakeholders. Much of the most interesting work arises from such applied research. On the other hand, I am struck by the way that the research grant system enshrines a scientistic model of scholarship. The applicant proposes a project that is designed to create new knowledge. It defines the problem, surveys the existing state of knowledge, outlines the methodology, the data to which it will be applied, the expected outcomes, and their national benefit. This suits researchers in the laboratory disciplines, and many researchers in the humanities adapt it to their needs; but it is less well adapted to reflection, reinterpretation, critical inquiry, and other forms of scholarship. Humanists have imitated that form of research, but it is an approximation of their fundamental purpose.

Indeed, there are reasons to question the adequacy of the present arrangements in supporting key disciplines and this applies across the disciplines. Policy measures to increase enrolments in the basic sciences (see Robb & Bullen, this volume) are yet to be reflected in student numbers (Macintyre, 2001). Some of our ablest mathematicians are leaving Australia to pursue their careers while too many Australian researchers have chosen to conduct their work in applied areas downstream from the basic research on the genome in the belief that the competition will be less keen. Without first-rate pure research, our applied research will be parasitic and insecure.

The humanities, too, suffer from a contraction in basic research. Anthropologists, for instance, have applied their disciplinary skills with considerable success, so that medical anthropology has become a major field, while work on Papua New Guinea and the Pacific has dwindled alarmingly. Likewise, the largest philosophy department in Australia, at Charles Sturt University, has 560 equivalent full-time students. Most of them are trainees for the New South Wales police force, since their degree course includes a study of applied ethics. This has benefits for both the police and philosophy, but the employment of ethicists does little for other branches of philosophy such as metaphysics. Applied philosophy thrives but other fields struggle.

In Canada, meanwhile, questions have been raised about programs in the social sciences and humanities which are "surplus" to the needs of the knowledge economy (Axelrod, Anisef, & Lin, 2001). In Australia, disciplines afflicted by low enrolments are advised to outsource to other universities. One policy document commends the practice of "Monash [which] is now teaching Russian to University of Melbourne students and the University of Melbourne [which] is teaching Ancient Greek and Latin to Monash students" (Nelson, 2002, pp. 29–30). Clearly, the Australian government does not see the attainment of a "critical mass" of researchers in these disciplines as a research priority. In this instance, critical mass is not so much an issue of whether or not such disciplines can be competitive in the global knowledge economy, but of the survival of fundamental disciplinary knowledges (see Hainge, this volume).

My final example is the teaching of languages other than English. In 1999 a working party headed by Professor Anthony Low undertook a study that was particularly concerned with collaborative schemes for teaching languages. Its survey of Australian universities revealed an alarming attrition of face-to-face language teaching. Just one university in 1999 taught Hindi, and just two Vietnamese. There were significant shortcomings in the availability of Russian, Korean, and Arabic; the Classics were judged to be vulnerable. Even more alarming was the rapid abandonment of many community languages; between 1997 and 1999 thirteen of them were lost to Australian universities (Australian

Academy of the Humanities, 2000). This in turn has implications for area studies in history, politics, literature, and other disciplines.

Much language teaching is conducted by small groups of staff, with heavy workloads, and with consequent implications for their research. Some of them fill out their curriculum vitae with work on language acquisition, but the research that grounds languages in their historical, literary, and cultural contexts languishes. The research record in linguistics is much stronger, but linguistics has also moved into applied forms of teaching in ESL, language testing, and so on. Yet the quality of work in applied ethics or language testing will depend upon strong departments of philosophy and linguistics.

*Conclusion*

The modernization of the traditional humanities disciplines has seen adaptation to new forms of research and movement into new fields of research opened up by the knowledge economy, assisted by new forms of research support and despite some barriers erected to the participation of the humanities. The preservation of these disciplines has required a range of survival strategies including application of their expertise. My concern is with the intellectual capital, the maintenance of the intellectual infrastructure, the opportunities for research training, the preservation of staff levels, and the affirmation of the values of the humanities.

While the university is part of the knowledge economy, its functions go well beyond it. As a teaching institution, the university seeks to satisfy the unprecedented increase in demand for higher education, and to ward off or accommodate the challenge of new providers and new technologies. As a research institution, the university seeks to capture the unprecedented growth of investment in knowledge creation. As a place of learning, the university struggles to maintain its responsibilities for scholarship, critical inquiry, and the maintenance of cultural tradition.

*Notes*

1. The demarcation between the humanities and the social sciences is imprecise. The Australian Academy of the Social Sciences includes historians, philosophers, and linguists. The panel of the Australian Research Council that funds research in the humanities and creative arts encompasses criminology, law, archaeology, and anthropology but not sociology or geography. As universities have amalgamated traditional disciplinary departments into conglomerate schools and interdisciplinary research centers, the traditional boundaries have blurred further. For this reason, this chapter frequently refers to the social sciences in its discussion.

## References

American Academy of the Arts and Sciences (2003). Humanities indicators, available online http://www.amacad.org/projects/indicators.htm

Asian Studies Association (2002). *Maximizing Australia's Asia knowledge: Repositioning and renewal of a national asset: A report.* Bundoora, Victoria: Asian Studies Association of Australia.

Australian Academy of the Humanities (2000). *Subjects of small enrolment in the humanities: Enhancing their future.* Canberra: Australian Academy of the Humanities.

———. (2003). *The humanities and Australia's national research priorities.* Canberra: Department of Education, Science and Training.

Australian Research Council (1998a). *Challenges for the social sciences and Australia.* Canberra: Commonwealth of Australia.

———. (1998b). *Knowing ourselves and others: The humanities in Australia into the 21st century.* Canberra: Commonwealth of Australia.

Axelrod, P., Anisef, P., & Lin, Z. (2001). Against all odds? The enduring value of liberal education in universities, professions and the labour market. *Canadian Journal of Higher Education, 31* (2), 47–78.

Bauman, Z. (1997). Universities: Old, new and different. In A. Smith & F. Webster (eds.), *The postmodern university: Contested visions of higher education in society* (pp. 18–26). Buckingham, UK: SRHE & Open University Press.

British Academy (2002). The British Academy in 2002, *The British Academy 1902–2002: Some historical documents and notes,* available online http://www.britac.ac.uk/pubs/src/ba-history/ba2002.html

Commonwealth of Australia (2001). *Backing Australia's ability: An innovation action plan for the future.* Canberra: Commonwealth of Australia.

European Commission (2002). *The Sixth Framework Programme in brief,* available online http://europa.eu.int/comm/research/fp6/pdf/fp6-in-brief_en.pdf

Gardner, W.J. (1979). *Colonial cap and gown: Studies in the mid-Victorian universities of Australasia.* Christchurch: University of Canterbury Press.

Jones, B. (1995). *Sleepers, wake! Technology and the future of work.* Melbourne: Oxford University Press (first published 1982).

Kenway, J., Bullen, E., & Robb, S. (in progress). *Haunting the knowledge economy.*

Kerr, C. (1963). *The uses of the university.* Cambridge, MA: Harvard University Press.

Macintyre, S. (2001). Traditions. In Department of Education, Training and Youth Affairs (ed.), *National Humanities and Social Sciences Summit, 2001, Position papers* (pp. 65–74). Canberra: Commonwealth of Australia.

Macintyre, S. & Marginson, S. (1999). The university and its public. In T. Coady (ed.), *Why universities matter: A conversation about values, means and direction* (pp. 49–71). St Leonards, NSW: Allen & Unwin.

Marginson, S. & Considine, M. (2000). *The enterprise university: Power, governance and reinvention in Australia.* Cambridge: Cambridge University Press.

Nelson, B. (2002). *Higher education: Report for the 2002 to 2004 triennium.* Canberra, Commonwealth of Australia.

Pascoe, R., Ainley, J., Macintyre, S., & Williamson, J. (2003). *The lettered country*. Canberra: Australian Universities Teaching Committee.

Poynter, J. & Rasmussen, C. (1996). *A place apart. The University of Melbourne: Decades of challenge*, Carlton South, Victoria: Melbourne University Press.

A. Smith & Webster, F. (eds.) (1997). *The postmodern university: Contested visions of higher education in society*. Buckingham, UK: SRHE & Open University Press.

Wagner, A. (1998). *Redefining tertiary education*. Paris: OECD.

———. (2003). Global perspectives on higher education. In Forum for the Future of Higher Education (ed.), *2003 Forum Futures* (pp. 53–56). Cambridge, MA: Forum for the Future of Higher Education.

·4·

*Greg Hainge*

# THE DEATH OF EDUCATION, A SAD TALE (DEST): OF ANTI-PRAGMATIC PRAGMATICS AND THE LOSS OF THE ABSOLUTE IN AUSTRALIAN TERTIARY EDUCATION

According to Derrida, in his 1991 address to UNESCO,[1] "philosophy is everywhere suffering, in Europe and elsewhere, both in its teaching and in its research, from a limit that, even though it does not always take the explicit form of prohibition or censure, nonetheless amounts to that, for the simple reason that the means for supporting teaching and research in philosophy are limited" (2002, pp. 14–15). He continues:

This limitation is motivated—I am not saying justified—in liberal-capitalist as well as in socialist or social-democratic societies, not to mention in authoritarian or totalitarian regimes, by budgetary balances that give priority to research and training that is, often correctly, labelled useful, profitable, and urgent, to so-called end-oriented sciences, and to techno-economic, indeed scientifico-military, imperatives. For me, it is not a matter of indiscriminately contesting all of these imperatives. But the more these imperatives impose themselves—and sometimes for the best reasons in the world, and sometimes with a view to developments without which the development of philosophy itself would no longer have any chance in the world—the more also the right to philosophy becomes increasingly urgent, irreducible, as does the call to philosophy in order precisely to think and discern, evaluate and criticize, philosophies. For they, too, are philosophies, that, in the name of a techno-economico-military positivism—by looking toward a "pragmatism" or a "realism"—and according to diverse modalities, tend to reduce the field and the chances of an open and unlimited philosophy, both in its teaching and in its research, as well as in the effectiveness of its international exchanges.[2] (2002, p. 15)

Whilst Derrida's declarations here issue from the French context, they no doubt resonate strongly with all those currently working within the humanities. It is Derrida's intention in this essay to recommend that we "displace" the teleological axis of philosophical discourse from its Greco-European origin or memory "by going beyond the old, tiresome, worn out, and wearisome opposition between Eurocentrism and anti-Eurocentrism" (2002, p. 9). Only by doing this can philosophy itself be affirmed not merely as a discipline but as a basic, inherent—although not of course teleological—principle of the university. As Derrida points out, to argue that philosophy is a basic principle of the university conforms with Schelling's conception of the university as "nothing but a large philosophical institution" (quoted in Derrida, 2002, p. 15). We can also see in this a fundamental right to philosophy which "is dissociable from a movement of effective democratization" (Derrida, 2002, pp. 5, 14). For Derrida, then, the very conditions of possibility for philosophy would today seem to depend on its ability to navigate between two poles, one abstract and seemingly universal, the other pragmatic and situated. Thus, as Derrida writes,

> it is not a matter of promoting an abstractly universal philosophical thought that does not adhere in the body of the idiom, but *on the contrary* of putting it into operation each time in an original way and in a non-finite multiplicity of idioms, producing philosophical events[3] that are neither particularistic and untranslatable nor transparently abstract and universal in the element of an abstract universality. (2002, p. 12, original emphasis)

At the same time as philosophy must affirm its absence of a single, univocal origin or place, then, this apparent universal or cosmopolitical must be kept in check by its local conditions. These local conditions, very often, are made manifest in philosophy's institutional embodiments. As Derrida notes, "although philosophy does not amount to its institutions or pedagogical moments, it is obvious that all the differences in tradition, style, language, and philosophical nationality are translated or incarnated in institutional or pedagogical models, and sometimes even produced by these structures" (2002, p. 12).

Derrida argues that philosophy needs to leave behind any Eurocentric or oppositional tendencies it may have, precisely because they are anathema to the very essence of philosophy. It could be argued, however, that to even talk of the university as a philosophical body is a privilege born of the very "cultural, colonial, or neo-colonial dialectic of appropriation and alienation" from which philosophical formations are supposed to be freeing themselves (Derrida, 2002, p. 10). In Australia at the present time, as with other OECD nations, to talk of the university as an institution that, like the exemplary model of UNESCO that Derrida proposes, is "a properly philosophical space and place" is completely to disregard our local conditions. At the present time it is perhaps not feasible even to consider our universities as properly educational, let alone philosophical (2002, p. 5). As a way of clarifying this extremely (and deliberately) controversial statement we need now to turn to education understood in terms of Derrida's work on "forgiveness."

## Forgiveness

In another address by Derrida, published in English as "On forgiveness,"[4] Derrida argues for a conception of forgiveness that holds an unconditional purity at its core at the same time as it is mediated by "the order of pragmatic conditions, at once historical, legal, political and quotidian which demand that the unforgivable be forgiven, that the irreconcilable be reconciled" (Critchley & Kearney, 2001, p. xi). This double movement is of course akin to that seen in Derrida's view of philosophy and the university. These two poles or orders of the unconditional and the conditional are, as Critchley and Kearney point out, "in a relation of contradiction, where they remain both irreducible to one another and indissociable" (2001, p. xi). As a result, as they continue, "responsible political action and decision making consists in the negotiation between these two irreconcilable yet indissociable demands" (2001, pp. xi–xii). On the one hand Derrida asserts that "in principle, there is no limit to forgiveness, no *measure*, no moderation, no 'to what point?'" (Derrida, 2001, p. 27)—a conception of forgiveness far removed from the common or dominant axiom of tradition for which "*forgiveness must have a meaning*" (Derrida, 2001, p. 36, original emphasis). On the other hand he is also obliged to recognize that even though "it should engage only absolute singularities, it cannot *manifest* itself in some fashion without calling on a third, the institution" (Derrida, 2001, p. 48, original emphasis). Herein lies the problem, for the institution, more often than not if not invariably, has a very different *modus operandi* than this ideal middle ground situated in the unavoidable aporia of an irreconcilable condition. The institution privileges pragmatic concerns, radically alters the nature of forgiveness, and in the process destroys it. Derrida writes:

> I shall risk this proposition: each time forgiveness is at the service of a finality, be it noble and spiritual (atonement or redemption, reconciliation, salvation), each time that it aims to re-establish a normality (social, national, political, psychological) by a work of mourning, by some therapy or ecology of memory, then the "forgiveness" is not pure—nor its concept. Forgiveness is not, it *should not be*, normal, normative, normalising. It *should* remain exceptional and extraordinary, in the face of the impossible: as if it interrupted the ordinary course of historical temporality. (Derrida, 2001, pp. 31–32, original emphasis)

Are these not the tenets of education for any good pedagogue? Do we not believe that education has the capacity to interrupt the ordinary course of historical temporality, that many of the radical breaks in human history that have appeared through massive social change or technological innovation have often been (at least in part) the result of education? Do we not believe that the role of education—if we conceive of this term in its purest sense—should also *not* be normal, normative, and normalizing but rather exceptional, extraordinary, and *inspirational*? If we do believe this then, like forgiveness, education also, in principle, has no limit, no *measure*, no moderation, no "to what point?" It has an unconditional purity, yet one that of course must negotiate the middle ground between this apparent absolute and the empirical, pragmatic pole because of its inescapable reliance on an institution for its becoming manifest. Our task now is to test current knowledge economy policies against this middle ground between these two irreconcilable positions.

## A Local Example

Australia has witnessed, along with other OECD countries, a rapid expansion of government policies that attempt to reconfigure higher education along lines suitable to a knowledge economy. We can examine how these policies fit within the space between the absolute and pragmatic conditions of education by looking at an example (typical of global knowledge economy policies) from the Australian Federal government's department of education, now known under the acronym of DEST. The particular policy document we will examine is entitled *Knowledge and Innovation: A Policy Statement on Research and Research Training* (Kemp, 1999). At first glance this document's pronouncements on the role of universities to "inspire and enable individuals to develop their capabilities to the highest potential throughout their lives" and other statements promoting the concept of lifelong learning seem to posit a model of education as something that has no limit (Kemp, 1999, p. 2). Likewise the document's pronouncements on the advancement of knowledge and understanding seem to posit education as an absolute value in itself. Indeed, does it not explicitly state that our universities should be places where "knowledge is valued for its own sake" (Kemp, 1999, p. 5)? The policy does indeed proffer *some* such statements of the absolute, yet at every turn this document, as well as governmental policy in general (and more and more so) enforces a pragmatic end upon education that leaves us, in the final analysis, not with education but training. As Stuart Macintyre has written, "the emphasis on industrial innovation and economic efficiency, pursued in the short time horizon of market returns, reorients the teaching function from education to training" (2001, p. 57). In this context the notion of lifelong learning (one of the key foci of knowledge economy policies globally) is a complete misnomer for this supposedly continuous accrual of knowledge as an end in itself (which would seem to be a properly philosophical goal). Lifelong learning for a knowledge economy is, rather, a start-stop operation that moves from one short-term goal to the next, a new pragmatic rationale for the continuation of education needing to be found at each successive step. Indeed, this politics of pragmatism has, as Macintyre notes, called into question every function of the university and led to a series of radical changes. What we are witnessing is the privileging of an imposed pragmatics of education and the suppression of its other, necessary aspect: an education "based on a movement of universality that exceeds the pragmatic demands of the specific context" (Critchley & Kearney, 2001, p. xii).

It is, of course, easy to criticize and far more difficult to propose possible pathways that will lead to a new and different construct to take the place of what is removed by de(con)structive criticism. To propose such pathways, however, is a necessary step, for any deconstructive practice can only be justified if it opens out a whole new realm of possibilities. So what can be done? How can education be reinvested with a sense of absolute purity to counterbalance the excessive pragmatism under which it is currently suffering and suffocating? It is not simply a question of asserting the absolute value of education, of overprivileging this absolute purity. As Critchley and Kearney write, "unconditionality cannot, must not . . . be permitted to programme political action, where decisions could be algorithmically deduced from ethical precepts" (Critchley & Kearney, 2001, p. xii). Rather, we need to propose a model that situates itself between the two poles of the problem—and is born of their tension.

In order to do this, I shall not have further recourse to Derridean philosophy lest it be thought that I am claiming his thought as the sole guardian of the possible answers for our problems since this would contradict the very kind of problem solving Derrida advocates. Rather, I shall take up Derrida's challenge to philosophy to return to its true, multiple essence and allow different voices from various areas of my research to create a "bastard, hybrid, grafted, multilinear, and polyglot" discourse (Derrida, 2001, p. 10).

## Immanence

Firstly, then, let me elaborate a concept taken from the philosophy of the thinker who informs my own work more than any other, Gilles Deleuze. Deleuze's philosophy is situated in a post-structuralist tradition (if indeed there is such a thing). Such tradition proposes an immanent critique of the world in the belief that no one term in any system can be taken as a transcendent ground to explain the entirety of that system. This critique holds the belief common to a long lineage of thinkers from Nietzsche to Spinoza to Marx that a whole or totality of any system cannot be given but rather remains open, constantly becoming. The totality of any system, then, can only be conceived of as a plane of immanence, a plane with no form or substance as such, only function and that is, as Brian Massumi has written, "a continually changing, turbulent pool of matter-energy" (1992, p. 170, n.4). Pure virtuality, this plane of immanence, pure outside or abstract machine, as Massumi goes on to note, is "outside our space of relatively stable matter and quantifiable energy"; it is a "pure outside, an outside so far out that it would have no 'itself' of any kind to be 'in'" (1992, p. 170, n.4). If we are to propose a model of education that situates itself between the two poles suggested by Derrida, in the tension born of the seemingly oppositional conflict of an absolute purity and an empirical pragmatics, then we could do worse than perceive of education as just such a plane of immanence or abstract machine—a term that is itself situated in the tension of the in-between of these two poles, both abstract (pertaining therefore to an absolute, a formless mass that is only *massive*) and machinic (eminently pragmatic, in other words, serving only to enact a function). It may at first seem that the plane of immanence is a concept that errs wholly on the side of the absolute, a transcendent concept, therefore. However, for Deleuze it is this very absolute purity of the outside that keeps his philosophy grounded in pragmatic concerns since philosophy no longer constitutes a science able to contemplate the real, pragmatic world from a privileged "philosophical" perspective. Rather, philosophy springs from the very same plane as empirical, pragmatic reality, thereby creating a transcendental empiricism, as Deleuze and Guattari (1987) term their own mode of thought.

In short, and in the terms of the present discussion, this means that the mode of pragmatic governance of any system is inherent and immanent to it.

Whilst it is no doubt true, then, that a sense of the absolute (be it ethical, moral, or whatever) *and* a pragmatic sensibility are required for the successful functioning of the university in the modern world, our mistake is in believing that these two poles are separated from each other, that a pragmatics needs to be imposed upon education from the outside. When the axioms imposed upon any system are external to it and not immanent, there can arise only a massive scene of neo-colonial conflict between those living within the system and those attempting to govern it from without.

Current knowledge economy policies make precisely this mistake, for education is consistently put in the service of an external axiomatic, namely income generation. Whilst it might be argued that this is merely a cry specific to the humanities for whom the paths to income generation are less apparent, I believe that it is a mistake for the sciences also to obey such an obvious pragmatic end. Doing so unavoidably means that one's research is motivated and guided by factors other than those internal to the research itself. This is a dangerous route indeed for universities which state that they will, amongst other things, harbor teachers, researchers, course designers, and assessors committed to *free* inquiry and the systematic advancement of knowledge.

This is not to say by any means, of course, that research within our educational institutions cannot or should not generate income. It means, rather, that it should do so only as a secondary effect, when there are evident, marketable outcomes arising from the untainted research carried out. This means also, however, that research and education should not *have* to obey this particular pragmatic, that income generation is not the only way for research and education to play a pragmatic role in society. A good education, one that obeys an absolute immanent in the very principle of education, will necessarily instill our future citizens with pragmatic tools with which to build a better society. To those for whom this seems like an overly abstract and resolutely anti-pragmatic statement, I would suggest that ultimately it is no less abstract than a belief that pragmatic value can be found in monetary return, for the liberation of surplus value upon which the entire capitalist edifice is founded is itself a very abstract concept. In order to found a pragmatic education, therefore, it is necessary only to assert the absolute value of education, to assert that education has a place in our society and must then be funded appropriately.

With regard to the specific pragmatics of the higher education sector, then, what action is required by this need for an absolute in the governance of our institutions that would allow them to be educational institutions once again? Quite simply, I believe that the answer lies in our research. I believe that if a large portion of state funding of higher education were dependent on the publication, *in whatever form is appropriate for each discipline*, of rigorous, scholarly work, then the experts employed by our institutions would be able to dedicate themselves to the pursuit and dissemination of knowledge. Our job as educators is precisely this, even if in the present climate this job description seems but a faraway ideal, a utopian dream. As long as knowledge economy policies are dictating modes of activity that are not immanent in the system under governance, a massive amount of redundancy is created. A huge surplus expenditure of energy (and indeed resources) is wasted on the performance of tasks that have nothing to do with the primary objective of an educational institution.

This redundancy can be seen in the weeks spent developing applications for research grants for projects that may not actually need anywhere near the level of funding requested. This redundancy is also evident uniquely in the ever-increasing layers of administration required to coordinate and live with the after effects of the so-called rationalization of academic departments or the seemingly unstoppable growth of infrastructure, process, and personnel required to gauge the quality of what we are doing—if we even know what we are supposed to be doing any more. Redundancy can also be found in knowledge economy policy itself, and is due once again to the loss of an absolute in the government's perception of education. To further this discussion of the presence of redundancy in knowledge economy policy I will now turn to a discussion of noise.

### Interference

In order to clarify this position and in the interests of continued hybridity, polyglotism, and bastard discourse, allow me briefly to talk about another area of my research: noise. Noise, conceived of theoretically, I contend, can be perceived as an absolute outside. White Gaussian noise, for instance, contains all sonic frequencies and is, then, the plane of immanence of all sonic events for it is the totality of potential sonic events, events that can come into being through the intensification of any of the infinite possible points of the plane or combination of such points. Yet noise is also, both for traditional communications theory and for the public in general, something that is undesirable, a by-product of the primary process of the various machinic entities that surround us. Noise, then, is perceived as something to be attenuated or eradicated; indeed, for communications theory it is that which disrupts the flow of information from source to destination. In order to combat noise, communications theory advocates the use of redundancy, an overstating of the original signal, if you will, in order that enough of the original signal reaches its destination untainted so as to remain comprehensible in terms of its original. We can see this same process in knowledge economy policy with respect to higher education.

The *Knowledge and Innovation* policy document is filled with redundancy for it is an attempt to vanquish the absolute of education (its noise, in other words) in favor of a supposed pragmatics. Indeed, much of this policy consists of redundant statements that explain the function of a university as if its role required clarification, a move akin to supplying a seasoned waiter with an instruction manual for his trusty corkscrew. This document is indicative, then, only of the massive gulf that currently divides external political thinking and internal academic thinking on the function of universities. Most academics I know do not need a document that tells them that "our universities have a crucial role in the national research and innovation system," and that "they are major contributors to the generation and transmission of knowledge in Australia" (Kemp, 1999, p. 2). The only reason most of them are still in the sector is because they know deep within them that they can "inspire and enable individuals to develop their capabilities to the highest potential throughout their lives," that they "advance knowledge and understanding," and that by so doing they "enable individuals to contribute to a democratic, civilised society and promote the tolerance and debate which underpins it" (Kemp, 1999, pp. 2, 3). So why do these absolute values of education need stating?

The answer comes in this document's section 1.5 entitled "A direction for change" and in which there is indeed a change of direction. This new direction, for which this document is I suppose intended as a map, leads us to talk of GDP and trade, competitive industries, sustainable economic growth, science and technology linkages, commercial settings, industrial environments, a national innovation system, economic benefit, commercialization, training, funding, strategically targeted research, business needs, private investment, emerging opportunities, investment and rewards, revenue streams, royalty benefits, equity shares, venture capital, reform of the taxation system, overseas pension funds and domestic superannuation funds, a pooled development fund, capital gains tax, venture capital projects, and corporate taxation. It suggests that we are to capitalize, be rewarded, be entrepreneurial, and to reinforce cycles of opportunities. All of these terms come within the first 67 lines of this section. The remaining thirteen lines offer platitudes disguised as absolutes that claim "the Government wishes to maintain Australia's performance in basic research and to ensure our universities remain places where creativity and discovery are fostered and knowledge is valued for its own sake" (Kemp, 1999, p. 5). In these final lines there is also an acknowledgment that "to do other than this would not only undermine the fabric of our institution, but may result in research graduates who are lacking in the vision necessary for knowledge breakthroughs in all fields of endeavour" (Kemp, 1999, pp. 5–6). Yet the weight of corporate-speak preceding these final two paragraphs leaves one with the definite impression that the future direction in which we are headed is one that *will* undermine the very fabric of our institutions and that *will not* convert our talented researchers into the promised "ideas power-houses" (Kemp, 1999, p. 6).

The word "education" appears twice in these eighty lines, not in isolation designating one of our primary goals for the future, a signpost on this brave new road, but in the terms "the Australian higher education sector" and "Australia s [*sic*] higher education research system."

## Conclusion

It might of course be argued that the point of the policy document is not to talk about education, that it is specifically designed to provide a basis of future thinking about research and innovation. However, even when focusing on the research done by universities, the university should, I maintain, retain its status as an educational institution, for our research is linked to educational principles in a very direct way, forming the basis of what we teach our students. More than this, however, the dissemination of the results of our research should always, I believe, be carried out primarily as an educational exercise, one that *may* again have secondary and pecuniary effects *but which must stem from an educational imperative at the outset.* Knowledge economy policies such as *Knowledge and Innovation* damage the potential of our institutions as a whole by putting them at the service of pragmatic concerns that seriously compromise our research and desecrate the very foundations upon which the university is founded. Likewise they bring massive amounts of redundancy into the university system because of the disjunction created between models of governance and those being governed. It is the loss of absolutes that we need to attend to before our institutions seriously contravene some of the most basic academic principles to which we adhere.

## Notes

1. Derrida's 1991 UNESCO address was originally titled "The right to philosophy from the cosmopolitical point of view (the example of an international institution)." The translation of this address constitutes the first chapter of the English volume published under the name *Ethics, institutions and the right to philosophy* (2002). Its second part is a transcript of the roundtable discussion that engaged a revised form of this address delivered as a contribution to the first International Conference for Humanistic Discourses held in April 1994 and which prefaced its original title with the precision "Of the humanities and philosophical disciplines."

2. If the length of this quotation seems excessive, we can take consolation in the fact that it is nowhere near as long as the passages of Kant quoted by Derrida in this address.

3. A "philosophical event" refers to any knowledge-seeking activity that tends away from the already known, which holds at its core a desire to uncover new aspects of the world so as to expand its possibilities. In this respect, all discussion of philosophy should be extended beyond the narrow confines of a discipline-specific practice to encompass all disciplines and especially all humanities disciplines.

4. "On forgiveness" was originally a response to a number of queries put to Derrida by the intellectual journal *Le Monde des Débats* in 1999.

## *References*

Critchley, S. & Kearney, R. (2001). Preface. In J. Derrida, *On cosmpolitanism and forgiveness* (pp. vii–xii). London: Routledge.

Deleuze, G. & Guattari, F. (1987). *A thousand plateaus: Capitalism and schizophrenia*, trans. and foreword B. Massumi. Minneapolis : University of Minnesota Press.

Derrida, J. (2001). *On cosmpolitanism and forgiveness*. London: Routledge.

———. (2002). *Ethics, institutions and the right to philosophy*, trans. P.P. Trifonas. Lanham, MD: Rowman and Littlefield.

Kemp, D.A. (1999) *Knowledge and innovation: A policy statement on research and research training*. Canberra: DETYA/Commonwealth of Australia, available online http://www.dest.gov.au/archive/highered/whitepaper/report.pdf

Macintyre, S. (2001). Traditions. In Department of Education, Training and Youth Affairs (ed.), *National Humanities and Social Sciences Summit, 2001, Position papers* (pp. 65–74). Canberra: Commonwealth of Australia, available online http://www.detya.gov.au/highered/respubs/humanities/summit701.pdf

Massumi, B. (1992) *A user's guide to "Capitalism and schizophrenia": Deviations from Deleuze and Guattari*. Cambridge, MA: MIT Press.

*Linda Marie Walker*

# THE IMPOSSIBLE BEING BECOMES (POSSIBLY)

Humanities and arts research will sometimes deliver "difficult" work. Sometimes the difficulty of the work, the writing/research, is necessary. Arts and humanities cannot always be making the complex simple. Sometimes there are stages that research goes through, where the obligation to do work on behalf of others will fulfil itself as a complex textual surface. Because that is the surface of the environment the arts and humanities find themselves engaged with now, this essay enacts research as writing. It enacts an encounter with the difficult textual surface that the arts and humanities currently encounter. It also discusses the work of artist Patricia Piccinini, who works on/with the space between aesthetics and science much in the same way as, for example, Mary Shelley's *Frankenstein* worked on science through aesthetic means. This paper then is both a type of writing as research and a discussion of an aesthetic practice that produces a surface on which we can trace the contours of the ethical and epistemological concerns opening out in the knowledge economy.

The art practice of the Australian artist Patricia Piccinini gestures toward—in a committed and generative way—a creative intellectual position that moves (in an unsettled and unsettling way) within this science-humanity seam (seam as a working space, an interstitial space, in a chora/ological way). Piccinini tries to imagine the outcomes of "advances" in science (in this case medical technologies—genetic engineering and stem cell research). She tries to imagine what they might surface (appear) as—and she collaborates widely to realize her ideas:

Piccinini rejects the notion that artists should always make their own work, that art is somehow about the hand of God coming through the hand of the artist. "I could spend a lifetime being a car modeller or a sculptor, but I haven't because I'm not interested in the process," she says. "Some people . . . love layering the paint, but for me that's not really engaging." (Strickland, 2003, p. 17)

Her work "evolves" from using different expertises: computing, prototyping, molding, coloring (ambiences, logics, beats, rhythms).[1] This is not a making via methods of "combining and re-combining already formed wholes or parts," rather it is one that reaches its limit on one plane and then seeks out limits on other planes in order to continue to stay in the air, so as to see what might surface from the "thrown di(c)e." It cannot do this by keeping within known borders; the chance/risk is of course the coming-to-be of the unplanned, unforeseen, even, and probably, the grotesque (or what is judged "grotesque").

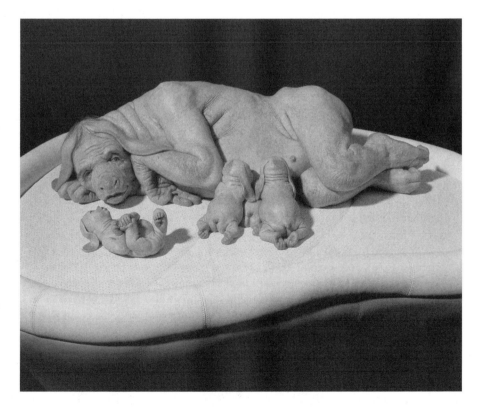

**FIGURE 1:** Patricia Piccinini, The Young Family (2002), silicone, polyurethane, leather, human hair, dimensions variable, *Photo: Graham Baring.*

The half-animal, half-human creatures she makes are disturbingly sympathetic.

> A fascination with science, medicine and abnormality has come to characterise Piccinini's work, much of it asking whether we will love the failures of such science as much as the successes. . . . "I wonder about [science's] potential to make our society intolerant to difference, to pathologise things. If you could make something to fix Alzheimer's that would be a cure, but if you made something to change black skin to white, would that be a cure? Or tallness? . . ." (Strickland, 2003, p. 17)

From the very start there is a question of "care." That is, to be care-less toward "the other," in whatever guise (be it person, thinking, writing, discipline, animal, substance), is already to be willing to exclude "the other," to eliminate their/its voice. This voice, call it "the humanities," call it "technology," call it "them," is within the common-world. It will always be intolerable to figure one voice over another. The conversation is the impossible possible (and it is most often effective in small moves, bit by bit—like here, like the fact that writing can only do small things—cannot, in other words, do everything, be everything, tell everything, cannot, in (more) other words, make sense (this is writing's baroque non-material inner-belly presence). It is the melancholy creature laying on the horizontal surface. The "conversation's" beauty and efficacy, its political and social work, is unknown, yet is always potentially "there," available, to sing out its "difficult gift." This "difficult gift" is its desire not to be already thought, not to confirm to a known form or shape or material (to be then of-its-own-kind as it comes about). The risk, aesthetically and technologically, is that "voice" will be together, in relation, in giving/receiving, and be the opening towards the other, an adventure.[2]

"The core of Piccinini's project," writes Juliana Engberg, Artistic Director, Australian Centre for Contemporary Art,

> is to give form to some of the concepts with which we currently grapple: those of scientific ethics and sociology. . . . Hers is a strange new world of unexpected places, populated by species of mythological creatures equally unexpected, yet somehow familiar. Myth becomes a form of reality in this world created by the artist from all that is material and potential in contemporary science and technology. (Engberg, n.d., p. 1)

Piccinini's creatures/beings (perhaps to be made-on-demand) are ambiguous on several levels: they are known yet other, mature yet infantile, calm yet anxious, communal yet insular, designed yet awkward. In her work we see something of our own ambiguous emotions concerning a

new science of commerce that perpetually shifts the frontier of consumer tolerance and desirability [that] has found ways to make cars, computers, and house-
hold appliances cute: part of the family—an extension of self—embodying physical attributes and emotional traits that reinforce the idea that our species
extends into technology and vice versa. (Engberg, n.d., p. 2)

And yet, at the same time, it is the humanities and the work of artists such as
Piccinini that must on all occasions be receiver, responder, keeper, complica-
tor, of what human beings do and make and bring into the realm of aliveness
(of all animate and inanimate communities); and strangely, even now, at this
very moment of preclusion it must (do its work) be its own defender and critic,
as if it were not itself, as if it were a stranger to itself. The idea of the humanities is coming to the surface through silence(ing), or through inattention.
This is, at this moment, its expression, its (potential) inventive motivation
(motion)—an involution, an (un)invitation to be present (to show its "drusy"
face[3]) amidst its own absence: a dreaming (work) out loud;[4] another type of
politics.[5] In light of new technologies, new economies, it must think both the
possible and the impossible; it, in itself, is new, an invention, by virtue of its
coming to the surface (newly born).

Invention is not a sovereign region (the sole preserve of a discipline) that
can be nominated. It is a process that is possible at any moment. (Teaching
teaches this: the student in design/arts is (can be) "invited" to put forward
something that the teacher does not know; here the teacher must learn what
evokes this "something," through what processes (research) the student ar-
ticulates/manifests this space/object.) Invention often comes through acci-
dents, mistakes, misunderstanding (for example, through students whose first
language [and therefore conceptual knowledge] is not English), impossible re-
quests, weaknesses in structure or argument, a change in the weather (and
weathering) (see for example Virilio, 2000).

Piccinini's deliberate mutations (interferences), appearances-in-process,
bodies of differing parts (a "wholeness folding into and out of fragmentation,
in composition of a surface of transformative continuity" [Massumi, n.d., p. 5]),
like "a pain in the eye" (Massumi, n.d., p. 12, quoting Pessoa), hybrid (inter-
species) "people" (pig, platypus, possum, rat), "organic lump siblings," are
there (arrived, still, mute), come about, not to intensify our dread, but to increase our tolerance for what can come about (surface without notice, fusion
or deformation beyond known desire or control), and (having arrived) touch
upon the ordinary, basic, issues (surfaces) of being human, being communal,
being loved and being loving, and how we might "feel" if each of these issues
becomes at issue with itself.

There is no straight line, smooth contour, or single point (here). There is no "clear" expression—the surface of the "matter" is not only spatial but temporal; and not only the-matter of the-fact; "matter" is derived from, or closely akin to, the Latin word mater—mother, maternal, producer—bringing us to the adjective "material," which can be defined as: "of bodily substance, of the perishable substance of the human body and of earthly things." In a sense, material is the mat(t)er(s) of the "earthly" world (Partridge, 1982, pp. 386–387)—and expression is, in the realm of sense, indeterminate, a spreading out, an endless surface surfacing; not simply a "flattening out" but "a power of combination, and as such [the creation of] the conditions for an art of unlimited encounter productive of a surface complexity: a complexity of interference" (Massumi, n.d., pp. 2–3). And it is the interference (the unexpected, the ludic, the momentary) that initiates, gives rise to, "the new."

With Piccinini, the quiet and accepting melancholic disposition of her creatures' surfaces, their monstrous selfhood, is evident and unclassifiable—we have no words for their mute state, yet they have come about, and we must speak. They change our thoughts, they invite another type of thinking, one that must be invented, with care: a surface transformation/transgression. The body of every surface is called into question; the situated time and space (where "I" am), the landscape of what something is—the seam between, for instance—and if something be-longs, and what it be-longs with, and how a be-longing response can proceed, has something to do with place and placelessness, with the thinking of the place of everything with everything else—the continual, continuous, inexhaustible exhausting surface.

The surface is a material presence, and also a non-material presence. The surface is not the oppositional interior outerness of the superior innerness (or structure). The imagination plays with the idea of everything being part of a continuous surface, everything in touch with everything else. Then, it appears (comes into thought) that the world and thought—how one is in the world—is infinitely formed by the touch of everything simultaneously (the way touch touches—then touch is surface, and surface transforms surface—as in conversation, which becomes a shape by response, by stuttering and stammering, by listening and remembering, by mishearing and mispronouncing, by laws and lawlessness, by ambient shifts and interventions: the surface of all the in-between surfaces and states changing themselves endlessly, sensuously—where a constant differing emerges independent and in-communion).

The surface appears (the surface/work of writing); I (we) attempt (and it is an endless attempt, as the surface never seems to completely surface) to attend to the-how of what appears in the world, as appearance, appears—whether material or immaterial, animate or inanimate: object/thing or subject/language. Another way of saying this might be that the surface, what is, as it comes to be, is "expres-

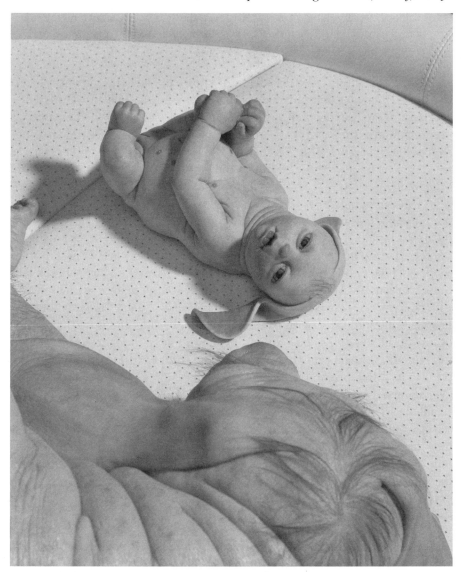

**FIGURE 2:** Patricia Piccinini, The Young Family (2002), silicone, polyurethane, leather, human hair, dimensions variable, *Photo: Graham Baring.*

sion," somehow, and everywhere; what comes about seems to come (about) by the events of expression; and these events are continual and "processual":

> The processual "surface" is all engulfing. It is active in and of itself. It is complex. In other words, it is a topological surface: of deformation and involution; of the

availability of every thing, of every form, even the ages of humanity (and the re-actions against them), to continuous transformation. Access to twisted excess. (Massumi, n.d., p. 5)

Within "all of this," the discussion of knowledge (whether art or science, and both), there is the strange pervading commonness of beauty. Underlying "understanding" (under our standing, our being (standing) in the world) is presentation (in time and space together and continual)—the coming-to-be-seen of the-appearing. And this "beauty" (that is again being thought about), is processual, is the everything of every-bearing-thing. (To repeat: "What is a thing judged beautiful, reevaluated from the point of view of beauty as process" [Massumi, n.d., p. 11]). "Every thing, however banal, is, and is beautiful, insofar as it is a bearer of otherness (that) and impinges (this)" (Massumi, n.d., p. 11). And impinging is an act on, upon, or against (rays of light impinging on the eye). To impinge "on" is to have/make (and this is without physical form or shape) an effect upon the surface of another thing/being, to have oneself felt, to feel, to sensate. An impingement is an impression; the impingement leaves a mark, a pressing into (an encounter given, received); and here memory and imagination unfold and twist, painful, ugly, rough, rude, and marvelous. "The beauty of the thing hits like a force launching a line of thought. Beauty impels thought. It compels thought. It is thought, contracted into the encounter, prior to its differentiation from sensation. All aesthetics is aesthetics of force" (Massumi, n.d., p. 12).

The passivity and acceptance with which Piccinini's beings present themselves is imbued with a type of force, an expression or exuding of themselves into their own particular and peculiar surfaces. They have come about painfully, in a sense, and we cannot ever get "inside" them (to the surfaces beneath the skin-depth of them), to feel what they might feel—we are forever present only with their presentiment, their complex (and foreboding) experimental surface, their aesthetic:

Aesthetic sensation is thoroughly synaesthetic. As thought unfolds from the sensitive encounter, the senses unfold from each other. The invited exploration is a co-functioning divergence of differentiating lines of further encounter, in the course of which an impossible world actually expresses itself, in a becoming-possible by degrees. (Massumi, n.d., p. 12)[6]

And this becoming-by-degrees is a method (and process) of thinking toward an exhausting and inexhaustive longing for be-longing-together within the consequences of prioritizing, of determining, or "inviting" particularized outcomes. It will be "the other" who is still here who will be making "itself" with the knowledge "it" gains by being studied as "other" by us—outside of production. This is, then, about hope. It is this impossible (other) world that Piccinini is making appear "by degrees," and which might be learning itself, by gazing back slowly.[7]

Jacques Derrida creates his essay "The university without condition" (in Derrida, 2002) as a complex (slow) surface, telling a story of the humanities that respects the past and respects the coming, if not the already-come, of a new humanities. It, as a questioning, querulous faculty, has probably always been its own inquirer, but times have changed; the aspect (condition) of question has transformed, and even though "the-question" is the domain of the humanities, it now is "the domain," as a question, that is the humanities "work." Derrida attempts to specify the "new" humanities—the humanities that one cannot give-up-the-ghost of/for:

> everything that concerns the question and the history of truth, in its relation to the question of man, of what is proper to man, of human rights, of crimes against humanity, and so forth, all of this must in principle find its space of unconditioned discussion and, without presupposition, its legitimate space of research and reelaboration, in the university and, within the university, above all in the Humanities. Not so that it may enclose itself there, but, on the contrary, so as to find the best access to a new public space transformed by new techniques of communication, information, archivization, and knowledge production. (Derrida, 2002, p. 203)

There is a question of how to proceed; a question of what the-making-of-knowledge is (this is not, for instance, "the" knowledge economy). This question is an inquiry: it is not simple, just as the surface is not, especially because it is mobile, unsightly, disorganized, violent, unstable. It is something to do with "understanding" sensed as multiple, self-relevant, banal, and complex— that is, horizontal, inclusive, and disordered, and this sense (sensorially) engenders, like interference, applications of unknown logics, geometries, makings (without prescription)—a kind of access (to excess) to the internal churnings (and limits thrown in the air) of expression. The making-of-knowledge is slow, it has little to do with "outcome" (outcome is possible, that is all—it is not mandatory).

Derrida's essay avoids no "encounter"—it advocates the "events" and "works" of the humanities, as productions of work: art, literature, music, theater. It brings to bear the very fabric of what the techno/sciences are bringing about: the "end of work." And, the fact that it is "the humanities" who will, must, think, philosophize, propose, debate, whatever, the repercussions/reverberations of "innovation" and "the commercialization of new ideas," it must be (follow), that sooner rather than later, "we" stop this mode of pitting things against things (we slow to think); work against work(s), and work with work. In this situation the essay does not set itself up in opposition, but relentlessly

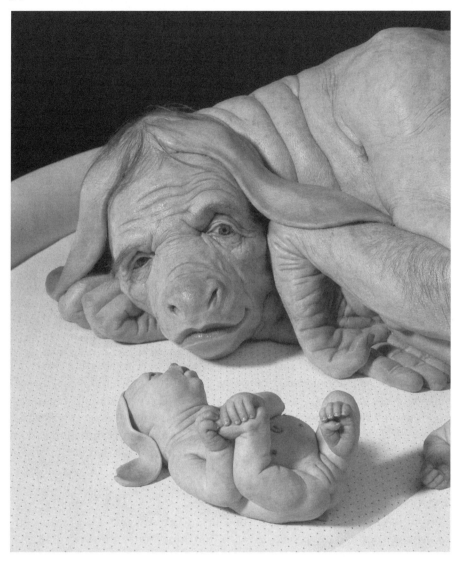

**FIGURE 3:** Patricia Piccinini, The Young Family (2002), silicone, polyurethane, leather, human hair, dimensions variable, *Photo: Graham Baring.*

sensitizes the idea of "resistance" necessary to "ask critical questions, not only about the history of the concept of man, but about the history even of the notion of critique, about the form and the authority of the question, about the interrogative form of thought" (Derrida, 2002, p. 204).

Disparity is necessary. Disparity creates (gives like the difficult gift) opportunities for collision.[8] From collision process moves—we do not know in which direction or toward what. In recent writings this banality of opportunity is called "beauty"—the beauty of things as they come about. ("Moving and opening, beauty pertains to a process that takes empirical precedence over the existing of formed things and their narratively closable coursings. 'Takes empirical precedence over form.' Or is it: takes deforming precedence over the empirical? A tectonic shift, ungrounding the ground of aesthetic experience" [Massumi, n.d., p. 2].) This is a turn of events, as the what-of-it of what-is is not an isolating or independent (judged as "something" at a distance) formation, but part of the composition of "a surface of transformative continuity, one-sided, asymmetrical, ontological twisting" (Massumi, n.d., p. 5). Silence, for instance, is crucial to noise; that is how we know the one and the other; but more than this, they are in themselves words for events of infinite difference, variation, brutal and delicate provocations.

And we say, would we dare, that the humanities are "beautiful." ("What is a thing judged beautiful, reevaluated from the point of view of beauty as a process?" [Massumi, n.d., p. 11].) It is "work," the idea of work, that is at stake here; the how and what of it; the what-to-call of it. When we make "works" we make a difference to the appearance of the world, however slight, banal, insignificant. When we question the sensibility of "beauty," for example, we bring into the light all possible surfaces, as well as "their work" in the world—all the surfaces of languages. Piccinini makes "express" a particular world driven by "what we might and might not" be able to love.

> Piccinini's work engages us because it does not take sides, though it draws from the conflicting emotions that underpin our fascination with genetic engineering. Her works give imaginative life to a potentially scary future, while also asserting the redemptive power of social values and relationships. Our horror of humans combining with other species, for example, is considerably softened or side-tracked by the image of Piccinini's profoundly weary and patient trans-species mother suckling her young. (Michael, 2003, p. 21)

It is, its image, at work, exuding, emitting; it is at work within the humanities. "What counts in the image is not its meagre content, but the energy—mad and ready to explode—that it has harnessed, which is why images never last very long" (Deleuze, 1997, p. 160).

*Notes*

1. "Among the specialists Piccinini works with are animatronics engineers, car modellers and upholsterers, 3-D computer animators, fibreglass form workers, sculptors and custom painters. Their everyday work may involve making sex aids and

animated puppets, or decorating hot-rods. Theirs are the arts of surface, making things for us to feel or photograph" (Michael, 2003, p. 10).

2. I touch upon Isabelle Stengers here, not in the complexity and subtlety of her thinking, but just to assist with the word "adventure": "I would say that the adventure of thinking is an adventure of hope. What I mean by 'adventure' is adventure as creative enterprise, in spite of the many reasons we have to despair" (Zournazi, 2002, p. 245).

3. "Beauty, [Kant] says, is 'drusy.' Or more precisely, our interest in beauty is awakened by drusiness. What in the OED is 'drusy'? A dusting of miniature crystals appearing on a surface: the sparkle of an appealing roughness that lures the eye to extend the hand. Although Kant does not explicitly comment upon it, this doubly returns us to process: once in the emergence of a surface disparity, and again in the relay from sight to touch" (Massumi, n.d., p. 6).

4. "By putting forward these questions, which still resemble virtual desires taken for realities, or at best barely serious promises, I seem to be professing some faith. It is as if I were engaging in a profession of faith. Some would say, perhaps, that I am dreaming out loud, while already engaging in a profession of faith" (Derrida, 2002, p. 214).

5. This politics could be what Isabelle Stengers calls

> an ecology of practices . . . it is about how different forms of knowledge and cultural practices work, but it is also the relation between what is happening and the way it defines itself in relation with others, or the way it represents those others. It is not concerned with individuals but with practitioners. I do not ask that scientists as people become better or more enlightened, I ask that practices stop ignoring each other, stop creating practitioners judging away what escapes their questions. (Zournazi, 2002, p. 262)

6. Christine Wertheim and Margaret Wertheim write about Piccinini's *The Young Family*:

> Wise and gentle, the mother's gaze seems human, as does the gesture of her arms. Her skin also is our skin, but those floppy, fleshy ears belong to no specific species, while the face is a hybrid of the human, the simian and the porcine. Most disturbing are her feet, and those of her pups, which resemble simian hands. Species boundaries are crossed here, but so are basic anatomical categories. Thus while The Young Family elicits a tender response it also incites a revulsion that we cannot entirely suppress; in part this is because we know—as Piccinini knows that we know—that science is currently bringing into being not dissimilar monstrosities, species spliced with features of unrelated organisms. Luciferase generating genes from fireflies have been transposed into tobacco plants, antifreeze genes from flounder have been inserted into tomatoes and frog genes into rhododendron plants. Hybridisation is our future. (Michael, 2003, p. 26)

Piccinini represented Australia at the 2003 International Biennale of Art, Venice, with an exhibition titled "We Are Family."

7. Isabelle Stengers:

> I am quite interested by the way American Indians put to good use anthropological knowledge and turn it into a political weapon. They learned about

us while we did think we were producing an objective knowledge about what defines them. The beautiful problem for human sciences, the problem for which we need a production of knowledge, is not what determines people or explains the way they think and feel, but the kinds of processes which may transform weak, isolated people into a collective able to invent its own position, its own strength. Again this is what I have called an "event". That is, we cannot think before something happens; if we anticipate it—if we claim we know beforehand what will take place and how—we destroy it, even by our goodwill. (Zournazi, 2003, p. 265)

8. The "difficult gift" is the unimagined one: loss, breakdown/up, friendship, love. For Clarice Lispector in *The Passion According to G.H.* (1998) it is a cockroach; for Hélène Cixous it might be the month of October ("In October 1991 . . ." in Cixous, 1998) or Clarice Lispector herself (Cixous, 1991); for Derrida (1995) it might be death.

## References

Cixous, H. (1991). *Coming to writing and other essays.* Cambridge, MA: Harvard University Press.

———. (1998). *Stigmata: Escaping texts.* London & New York: Routledge.

Deleuze, G. (1997). *Essays critical and clinical,* trans. D.W. Smith & M.A. Greco. Minneapolis: University of Minnesota Press.

Derrida, J. (1995). *The gift of death,* trans. D. Wills. Chicago: University of Chicago Press.

———. (2002). *Without alibi,* trans. P. Kamuf. Stanford: Stanford University Press.

Engberg, J. (n.d.) *The world according to Patricia Piccinini.* Melbourne: Australian Centre For Contemporary Art, available online http://www.accaonline.org.au/article?selector=conmap:371 (accessed 14 May 2003).

Lispector, C. (1998). *The passion according to G.H.,* trans. R.W. Sousa. Minneapolis: University of Minnesota Press.

Massumi, B. (n.d.) *Deleuze, Guattari and the philosophy of expression (involutionary afterword),* available online http://www.anu.edu.au/HRC/first_and_last/works/crelintro.htm (accessed 29 April 2003).

Michael, L. (ed.) (2003). *Patricia Piccinini: We are family.* Sydney: Australia Council.

Partridge, E. (1982). *Origins: A short etymological dictionary of modern English.* London: Routledge & Kegan Paul.

Strickland, K. (2003). Mother love. *Weekend Australian Magazine,* 3–4 May, p. 17.

Virilio, P. (2000). *A landscape of events,* trans. J. Rose. Cambridge, MA: MIT Press.

Zournazi, M. (2002). *Hope: New philosophies for change.* Annandale: Pluto Press Australia.

## ·6·

*Stephen Loo*

---

# CHOOSE TECHNOLOGY, CHOOSE ECONOMICS: THE ETHICO-AESTHETIC OBLIGATION OF THE ARTS AND HUMANITIES

> *The true, the good, the beautiful are "normalising" categories for processes which escape the logic of circumscribed sets. They are empty referents, they create a void, they install transcendence in the relations of representation. To choose Capital, the Signifier or Being, is to participate in a similar ethicopolitical option. . . . On the small scale, this redeployment can turn itself into a mode of entrapment, of impoverishment, indeed of catastrophe in neurosis. It can take up reactive religious references. It can annihilate itself in alcohol, drugs, television, an endless daily grind. But it can also make use of other procedures that are more collective, more social, more political.*
> (GUATTARI, 1992, P. 29, emphasis added)

I find myself obligated. This essay arrives out of a growing sense of obligation for the arts and humanities to attend to a new global knowledge economy seemingly underwritten by a techno-economic paradigm. The arts and the humanities are anxious about a future where knowledge is immanent in capitalist exchange and production, and where reductionist rationality prevails to provide the conditions for knowledge proliferation. That is, growth in knowledge, and therefore knowledge disciplines, is contiguous with commercial viability or exchange potential, augured by classical, objectivist, scientific theories. The fear is that scientific and technological knowledges will beat the arts and humanities to the economic finish line each time. What is in question here is the future for the arts and humanities: how do the arts and humanities attend to the coming being that is technological and economic? The question is therefore one of *belonging*—of how to belong; of "relations"—between the arts and humanities, and technology and economics.

The arts and the humanities are nevertheless already in action. A general purview shows that "cultural industries" such as media production—movies, newspapers, music—contribute widely to technological development and economic exchange. The "creative arts" continue to hold capital value, and open up technological domains through the use of digital and immersive technologies. There is also work produced in the humanities as "redemption" or "critique" of the techno-economic, for example work that preserves historical knowledge, provides a "sense of place," or maintains ethical values (see, for instance, Ruthven, 1998).[1] In these positions, however, the arts and humanities continue to play second fiddle to the techno-economic, either by their take-up of new technologies or the provision of theoretical commentary on the contemporary condition.

To what extent, then, can aesthetic practices become a generative force in the global knowledge economy, namely, the *genesis* or social production of creative subjectivity, found within the obligation to act in the new techno-economic world order? Through theoretical ruminations on "belonging" in the work of Giorgio Agamben, and the autopoetic nature of the aesthetic paradigm through Deleuzo-Guattarian philosophy, this chapter posits a deconstructed account of ethical action towards an alternative conceptualization of practice, which is strongly related to the concrete situations at the moment of its taking place; where creativity, as the creation of new concepts and subjectivities, is required.

## Belonging to the Coming Being

There is a sense of belonging, one we can reclaim with Giorgio Agamben, that focuses on a *belonging* together. Agamben (1993) posits belonging as attending to *whatever* comes (in the name of technology or capital) as being—*such as it is*. The aphorism does not advocate that the arts and humanities passively accept the fate that the global knowledge economy seems to imply is destined for them. Nor should the arts and humanities be indifferent to technology and capital because they are always already imbricated in the techno-economic. In *belonging* together, whatever (other) that comes "always matters," because such belonging occurs with desire, and will, as in be-*longing*. (The key term for Agamben (1993, p. 1) is "whatever," as he says "the coming being is whatever being." "Whatever" is the condition that is neither particular nor general. In Latin, whatever (*quodlibet*) contains the root *libet*, referencing the will, and relating to desire. That is, whatever comes is not met by indifference, but a desire for what it is, *as it is*.)

But whatever is it that comes? I return to my original obligation, where the question awaits: what or who is it that obligates (me)? Perhaps it is the urgent need for the humanities to deal with technological imperatives in research, to "be technological." Perhaps it is the call of capital, where disciplinary viability depends upon being commercial, profitable. Perhaps there is a "higher" imperative: to resist the anonymity and groundlessness of all that is technological and economic, swords that strike at subjective individuality. In other words, my obligation answers a call that comes from the heart of the humanities, to save something of beauty, namely the aesthetic of humanism. Perhaps then, it is the call to ethical action.

However, the heart of the matter here, now, is that I *find* myself, as the humanities *finds* itself, obligated to attend to technology and economics. Obligation always arrives uninvited and we are suddenly face to face with it. We are always at the receiving end of obligation. Unlike ethics, which works through principles to furnish judgements and actions in order to guard our sovereignty as a subject, obligation, to John Caputo (1993), challenges personal freedom, and as such shatters self-interest.

I fear that the obligation to act in the arts and humanities comes too readily, and appears too safe. Obligation overwhelms, as one finds oneself called to respond, without conclusion, so to speak, to the other that comes. It seems from the presentness-at-hand, or one can say the quickness, of the humanities' current responses to the global knowledge economy (like ready solutions to imposed problems), the techno-economic other is somehow already known, or can at least be named, in order to be gathered together in welcome. Herein lies the power of ethics, where a belief in the transcendental eschews the fear of the stranger and makes safe the call of obligation. There is faith that the "who" or "what" that obligates can be assimilated and become part of the family, and not remain the unknown. Ethics keeps obligation safe at home (see Caputo, 1993, pp. 5, 12); it names the stranger at the door, so that life at home does not become too difficult. It is a matter of "accommodation," as in "an alternative paradigm for these times needs to be able to accommodate technological and economic change as well as social, political and cultural change" (Bullen, Robb, & Kenway, 2004).

As a consequence, I fear that the social production of creative subjectivity, the fold into the ontological "I," occurs too quickly, because there exists some conventional sign of equivalence for exchange value between the techno-economic being that comes, and the arts and humanities who are obligated. This proportional equivalence of exchange assumes a law of needs (following Aristotle), or the communal substance of labor (following Marx), between the techno-economic and the arts and humanities, to maintain capital circulation towards the production of the social being. However—and this point will be developed later in the chapter—the central role previously occupied by the labor force in the production of surplus value for exchange is eroded by the convergence of speculative capital and invention in virtual production within the new world order, defying conventional laws of commodification. Capitalism now targets the matrix of emergence of both subjects *and* objects, thereby calling into question the determinacy of actual processes of social reproduction. Subjectivity is no longer the property of the individual, but is deterritorialized with the formation of the world itself.

Obligation, arriving unannounced as a "spontaneous causality, a cause without antecedent" (Caputo, 1993, p. 13), is such a moment of deterritorialization. The moment of obligation is a singularity. "I *find* myself, and the humanities *finds* itself, obligated." Obligation is; it happens; it is not willed, but stands a force from without. Local and grounded in the particularity of the moment, obligation bears an everydayness. As such, it possesses a definite materialism, and specific epistemological framework: there is technology and there is economics. In fact, the arts and humanities are obligated because technology and economics have already arrived at the moment of obligation. They are here and now: there is technology, and there is economics, at work and calling for a response. Note that this observation does not pre-empt the shape of the techno-economic. Technology and capital are not historically "given" at the moment of obligation, as they are themselves assemblages whose shapes are only given by the singularity of the event.[2]

Ethics would find it hard to survive in such an incomprehensible, unfree, and indeterminate event. In obligation, the transcendental does not feature, and there is no reconciliation with the other on the road to the Absolute; there is no Beauty. If anything, obligation is transcendence itself (Caputo, 1993, p. 27). Nevertheless, the hand of ethics continually attempts to smooth the territory, forcing knowledge to "economically" reconcile the object and the subject, the particular and the universal, interiority and exteriority. Technology and economics appear monolithic. It follows that in this closing movement of ethics, work in the humanities in the face of the techno-economic is arguably always already technological. This is because such work aims to *redress*—assimilate, temper, reverse, or eschew—what appears as other (in the case of the technological and the economic); for example, Hartley and Cunningham's (2001) reconciliation of dualisms of elite–mass, and art–entertainment, towards the formation of "creative industries." Reconciliation, like assimilation, involves recourse to a transcendent state under the aegis of progress, which may take the form of economic equality, political democracy, or socio-cultural equivocality, legitimating aesthetic practices in the humanities and creative arts for the future (Bullen et al., 2004). What drives redress is the same condition that drives technology: an ethical obligation to progress. Aesthetics becomes ethics.

The obligation to progress is well entrenched in the history of ethics as action based upon accepted norms with a well-rehearsed genealogy to the Good. The Good has since Plato been a key player in the history of metaphysical economies. The Good (or Absolute, Reason, Being, and the like) as universality of shared legitimacy and intelligibility, makes ethical judgement possible. It is the measure—the *arche* and *principium*—that holds all things in their place during the Hegelian subject's self-effectuation.[3]

Unfortunately then, the other invited home is no stranger, but one already mediated by technology, the greatest danger that already knows the home well. To say this in another way, the techno-economic is already technological when it appears; its otherness is already appropriated. The more the arts and humanities attempt to define the other, in welcome (in order to belong to it) within the safety of home (ethics), the deeper they become enframed by technology.[4] So, does work in the arts and humanities, in its obligation to attend to global knowledge economy policies, inescapably belong to technology and capitalism and is it therefore doomed not to be able to reveal the world in other ways?

### *Subjectivation as "Taking Place"*

If there is a way out,[5] it is at the moment of obligation, to which I return again. Attending to the singularity of obligation entails a very different kind of ethics, of what Agamben (1993, pp. 13–15) calls a "taking place." If the other is defined in advance of welcome, as found in the drive for completeness within the processes of assimilation, reconciliation, or redress, it leaves no room for alterity. All possibilities of impropriety have been, as mentioned, appropriated. The other is not coming; it has already arrived. In obligation, because belonging to the other is longing for its being—*such as it is*—the movement is not one of appropriation, and the relation is not of propriety, but of "opening" or giving "space" for the coming being, for the other to "take place." To Agamben, ethics begins only when the Good (authentic, true) is not a property over Evil (inauthentic, false) that is cast aside in appropriation, but is the showing of taking place of the Evil, the showing of its innermost impropriety. For the techno-economic (I am certainly not advocating that technology and economics are evil; but irreducibly other) to reveal other subject positions for the arts and humanities, it must be welcomed in its *coming*, its taking place, in fact as the "coming of the place to itself" (Agamben, 1993, p. 15). This place of taking place is perhaps Foucault's ineluctable "unformable and unformed Outside" (Deleuze, 1988, pp. 96–97; 112–113), the continuous arising of entities as knowledge–power relations, animated by movement and foldings. Taking place is a multiplicity (*hetero-*) that forms and reforms (*genesis*), meaning that the production of subjectivity is immanent in a *heterogenesis*, a territory of multivalent becomings at the intersection of the mentalistic, biological, semiotic, and machinic components. Emphasizing the processual, Deleuze and Guattari, following Foucault, speak of "subjectivation" rather than the precipitation of subjectivity. Subjectivation is the process of continual invention and production, in which the self *and* the other presuppose the existence of each other to produce themselves. In heterogenesis, components evolve and multiply, while maintaining their differences as difference. An example of this discussed by Deleuze and Guattari is the wasp and orchid where we see "the *aparallel evolution* of two beings that have absolutely nothing to do with each other" (1987, p. 10). While each component presupposes the existence of others for their subjectivation, all components remain strange to each other. The self can never be, or have full knowledge of, the other, but belongs to it *as it is*. With regards to the arts and humanities therefore, this should be the manner in which they respond: not reactively, but through a transversal affirmation of difference that is then necessarily a flowing toward the other.

The transversal relation between self and other in subjectivation has an implicit creative dimension as it contains processes that affirm an existential matrix of self-other at the moment of relation, by engendering other unforeseen and unpredictable modes of being: a re-poeticization, or (re)invention by reappropriation, of subjectivity. Guattari (1992, p. 34) calls this condition "machinic heterogenesis," neither to mean subjectivation behaving with evolutionary potential as that of a technical entity, nor an automatic (animalistic) one, but one which has "a singular power of enunciation," that is, the capacity to speak otherness into being, therein demonstrating its existentializing function.

The aesthetic is not marginalized by techno-economics. The latter confers upon aesthetics a key position in the intensification and self-affirmation of the humanities. The aesthetic paradigm is in effect autopoietic (Guattari, 1992, p. 106). Here, aesthetics moves away from the agential redress of the effects of technology and capital, proceeding from a position of disinterestedness of the other; to a practice of self-regeneration with an autopoietic consistency, which entails the unconditional welcome for the other. On the occasion of such welcome, the arts and humanities are irreducible to the taking place of the techno-economic; the latter is its innermost exteriority.

What are the implications of heterogenesis for practice within the arts and humanities in the face of the global knowledge economy? Herein lies a choice: either to assimilate or redress technology and economics in an obligation to progress that further enframes thinking, or to face the danger of the coming techno-economic being, to let it "come to pass." The second option is akin to what Guattari means by the ethico-political choice for Capital, Signifier, or Being. While the "redeployment" of transcendentals can turn into a mode of entrapment or impoverishment, Guattari holds hope that it could also open up other disclosures and procedures. It is the ultimate risk, but one that must be taken. Facing this risk requires a comportment that does not reduce the danger of choosing technology and choosing economics, but restores to danger its truth: the taking place of techno-economics that brings to sight what belongs to it (Heidegger, 1977). Note that technology and economics do not disappear and are not overcome in their coming to pass; nor is allowing the coming to pass of technology and economics a license for nonaction. The decision to obey or disobey such an obligation does not proceed through an adjudication of ethical principles, but is based on the effects of obedience or disobedience, what benefits or disasters the choice brings at the present moment (Caputo, 1993). It can be said that obligation is not rational; its authority is ambiguous, and its *logos* not wholly intelligible. To Guattari (1992, p. 28), the choice to obey is made at the level of feeling (*pathos*), as he says, "in pathic logic, there is no external global reference that can be circumscribed. The object relation is destabilised, and the functions of subjectivation are put into question."

Because of the autopoietic consistency in heterogenesis (Bains, 2002, p. 106), we alone take the ethico-political responsibility for our actions by the way we creatively posit new subjectivities, and reappropriate the means of their production. Heterogenesis offers a *place* that is not prior to action, but is itself a "place of action." We turn now to the work of Dutch architect Rem Koolhaas, not to describe his urban projects immanent in the contemporary techno-economic strata as exemplars, but as enactments, of the process of subjectivation, to hint at a difficult comportment to practice faced by the arts and humanities.

## *The Biopolitics of Rem Koolhaas' "Generic"*

*What is immediately striking is that the entire system of the PRD [Pearl River Delta] generates 300,000 square miles of urban substance per year.*
(KOOLHAAS, 2000, P. 312)

*Home Depot—the number three retailer in America—adds a new store on
average every 52 hours.*
(KOOLHAAS, 2000, PP. 536–537)

Let us consider a particular theoretical moment that seems to be an uncomfortable valorization of all that is technological and economical. The generic is a key concept in Rem Koolhaas' urban and architectural analyses. Koolhaas, whose prolific urban and architectural publications and significant corpus of built work has inspired a whole generation of contemporary architects and designers, is unapologetic about the reliance of contemporary urban development upon technology, and its immanence in the speculative flow of capital. In what are already modern classics (or have at least achieved cult status in architectural design disciplines) volumes such as *Delirious New York, S, M, L, XL,* and *Mutations* enact existential matrices in research and thinking within the humanities and the arts that herald the continual coming of technology and capital upon the scene.

Koolhaas uses images of unremarkable high-rise forms endlessly repeated, representing the American city; descriptions of infrastructure based on anthropomorphic allegories interspersed with advertisements from daily tabloids; and statistical comparisons relating to population density and land use in Asian cities. His theorizations ratify the production and appreciation of a kind of homogeneous, serial, and banal space, whose logic is unfettered by design or socio-cultural inscription. In the generic city, the production of architectural substance seems to proceed by accident at an alarming rate in a sort of aesthetic-free zone. The generic works at one level as documentary evidence, and thus symbolic representation, of how modernization has transformed the urban.

At another level, the generic is indeterminate: what the generic truly represents, and what is representative of the generic, is never arrived at. The generic does not lie solely as something referred to by, or immanent in, specific discursive or material instantiations. The material object that is the city is of no teleological consequence to Koolhaas. What appears, or what he *presents,* as the generic city—in finite form, as images, narrative, text—is propositional, because form here is governed by an economy of radical openness, which stems from the economy of the incomplete under the guise of representation. An impossibility exists in form operating under representation, which is the overcoming of the absent figure desired by representation (Benjamin, 2000). Therefore, what the generic, as a theoretical construct, precipitates as finite form are propositions that attempt to close the gap between the figure and its representation, maneuvers that are necessarily futural that augur what-will-be or yet-to-come. In Koolhaas' work, actualizations of the generic at the nexus of, say, photo essays of seemingly inhumane (therefore "impossible" to western eyes) urban densities of Kowloon's Walled City (MVRDV, 1998)[6] or anthropological studies of shopping in America combined with analytical depictions of urban growth statistics (see Koolhaas, 2000; OMA, Koolhaas, & Mau, 1995) are deformities (excessive, accidental, or uncanny forms) within the processes of architectural production. On the surface, Koolhaas' theoretical work is very much part of the ordinary language of architecture. The resultant symbolic forms, as image, text or architecture, are not different from the accepted technological and economic codes of communicating architecture. But yet Koolhaas' language does not, or cannot, follow the logic of articulation of ordinary language because the premise of articulation itself, which is language's limit or border, is the unavailable figure of the generic. In this way, language in its imprecision is continually in excess of the symbolic.

Koolhaas' generic therefore goes beyond an aestheticization of the banal because the open nature of the generic establishes a generative potential. Appearing within slippery assemblages of language, design, and image, the generic augurs Agamben's coming being with a "whatever" existence. The generic, as the techno-economic being that comes, is bare abstraction, a substance disattributed from the hegemonic processes of urban production owing to its resistance to forestall the closure called for by representation. It possesses a structural potentiality that acquires the freedom to reactualize, or reattribute, in "whatever" determination. In relation to its immanence within the processes of subjectivation, therefore, the generic possesses the power to provide the freedom of choice for the creative repoeticization of modes of being. This is where work such as Koolhaas' presents the ground of the ethico-aesthetic paradigm within the arts and humanities. As Agamben (1993, p. 43) says,

> there is no essence, no historical or spiritual vocation, no biological destiny that humans must enact or realise. This is the only reason why something like ethics can exist, because it is clear that if humans were or had to be this or that substance, this or that destiny, no ethical experience would be possible—there would only be tasks to be done.

So far, the analysis of coming being has emphasized the "potentiality" of the generic, whether it actualizes this way or that, or not at all. Nevertheless, the generic in Koolhaas appears, and remains appeared, in finite form. There are two conditions that govern the generic as finite form. Firstly, depictions of generic urbanism arrive from somewhere; they belong to specific cultural conditions: the densities of East Asian cities, the *tabula rasa* approach to government-controlled development in Singapore, the American socio-geographical conditions that lead to the *mall*ification of shopping, and so on. In Koolhaas's work, the generic has been expropriated from bodies it rightfully belongs to, and as such contains traces or inscriptions of its former bodies. The generic therefore is not indifferent in the finite form it takes in publications, and is not indifferently attributable. It has a particularity in its genericity: Agamben's "whatever." The second governing principle is that the definition of the generic in finite form is *partial*, where the relations between form and the value of the generic are corrupted, or equivocal. This can be explained, in one way, through the lack of semiotic footholds within the language of Koolhaas' work. The speculative, exploratory, and at times errant,[7] nature of Koolhaas' theoretical language constantly dissimulates the metaphysical connection between language (text) and representation. His reliance on melancholic, sometimes wholly dreadful, urban images leaves the imagination with very little semiotic footholds to deal with evocations of loss within the hyper-reliance on technology and capital. The images are not linguistic or visual representations of loss, but are an affectual condition of loss themselves. Being in excess of symbolic or representational form brings forth the limit of language, not for the sake of transgression—Koolhaas' work is never really about seeking limits in order to permeate them—but allows partial (incomplete) definitions of form that have an ambivalent relationship to language. Through the lack of semiotic footholds Koolhaas' partial forms rely upon the surface of conventional language, all the while challenging the viability of symbolic instantiation itself, without falling into the closure demanded by representation.

The alteration between the two conditions of formalization—its particularity that appears as trace, and partial definition in finite form—in conjunction with the futurity implicit within the project of representation, allows the generic city to take on a radical speculative consistency. The generic can never be defined as here, now, for this or that purpose; it only survives in an anticipatory future mode: it will always be coming, and it will come only to shift its conditions of future possibility. Hence, it encounters no finitude or limit to its growth. The generic will continue to reproduce itself outside the limits of form, and will never stop exceeding itself because it speculates on its own future as something in excess of itself. The generic proliferates, expands, self-generates; it is a potentiality that escapes the law or non-contradiction.

It is evident from Koolhaas' example that Marx's productive labor is becoming increasingly immaterial, and that capitalist accumulation of value no longer follows a science of equivalence in the cycle of need, but spirals outwards in an ever-increasing and uncontrollable growth pattern. In their publication *Empire*, Hardt and Negri (2000, pp. 28–29) believe that there is an immediately communicative dimension in living labor that defies the productionist model of capital. While it is clear that Koolhaas' commentary on contemporary urbanism has had a profound effect upon recent approaches to urban design, in the West as well as in the East, and his built projects do not shy away from the hyper use of technology and its reliance on large capital expenditure, it is his publications that are media savvy and sustain their own expansive proliferation that spawned a new generation of communication engendered within the commodification of urbanity. The production of immaterial and speculative urbanity implicates processes of subjectivation at the level of an individual and of nation-states. Koolhaas' generic urban production is mobilized through the presentation of affectual states: the dread and loss in Asian urbanism in which the nightmare of western modernization comes true firstly challenges the West's conception of its techno-economic superiority, but simultaneously presents a premise for national identity negotiations by nation-states in the East, in relation to themselves, and to the West (see also Loo, 2002).

## Conclusion

Speculative capital no longer targets actual products, labor or services, but the matrix of emergence of the biopolitic before actualization; that is, the potential for new subjectivities. Foucault's structuralist epistemology is having a hard time dealing with the dynamic of the temporality of movements in a biopolitical society. Even the Deleuzo-Guattarian ontology of social production as machinic, which nevertheless highlights the horizons of language and communication, rarely delves into the relations between real bodies (corporeality) and value production. It will take an analysis through the work of communication theorists such as Brian Massumi (for example, 2002) to see how capitalism now relies on the production, manipulation, and circulation of the somatic, affectual, and corporeal (see also Hardt & Negri, 2000).

Koolhaas' work shows us an aesthetic practice that is not about aestheticization of finite forms of the generic, but an aesthetic practice in which the bare potentiality of the generic (incapable of taking significatory purpose or life) is reappropriated to become an "absolute biopolitical substance that, in its isolation, allows for the attribution of demographic, ethnic, national and political identity" (Agamben, 2002, p. 156). Agamben's substitutability resiles from universalizing the social, and creative subjectivity. Creativity comes in ways that capture the production of life itself, an autopoiesis, where the econosphere becomes the ontogenesis of the biosphere.

Aesthetic action cannot therefore be divorced from the moment of subjectivation, and is therefore no longer bracketed by idealism or autonomy. Aesthetic practice to Guattari "leads to a different type of re-enchantment of the expressive modalities of subjectivation" (Guattari, 1992, p. 105), highlighting it as a creative process that is necessary for ethical activity. The aesthetic paradigm, which is also an ethical one, moves towards new possibilities for thinking and acting in the (techno-economic) future. "New" here is not simply the reconfiguration or negation of something already known, but an encounter with something unthought (Zagala, 2002). Attending to the unthought is an obligation to the whatever being that comes, such as it is. Within subjectivation structured by the new global knowledge economy is an ethics and aesthetics of the arts and humanities.

## Notes

1. In my area of architectural research and practice, which straddles both the humanities and the sciences, the dominance of the techno-economic paradigm is clear. Backing, economic or otherwise, is readily available for scientific investigations into material performance, construction systems, facilities management, organizational behavior, and digital infrastructure.
2. Furthermore, the production of the new global order is decentralized, transgressing state boundaries and with plural networks of command, forming hybrid identities and flexible hierarchies of the techno-economic. See Hardt and Negri (2000, pp. xii–xiii).
3. Self-effectuation entails "assimilation" (to use a Platonic term) with the material world toward a higher status.
4. Herein lies a view of technology well worn through Heideggerian scholarship: technology is more than a tool amenable to vocational, commercial, and objective thinking; it is ontological as *techné* apprehends the univocal truth of being.
5. As Heidegger (1977, p. 42) says, quoting Hölderlin, "But where the danger is, grows, The saving power also."
6. MVRDV are Dutch architects highly influenced by Koolhaas, and were students of his. Their publication *FARMAX* follows closely in style and content precursors by Koolhaas such as *S, M, L, XL* (see OMA, Koolhaas, & Mau, 1995).
7. Koolhaas himself admits that "there is an enormous, deliberate, and—I think—healthy discrepancy between what I write and what I do" (see Heron, 1996, online).

## References

Agamben, G. (1993). *The coming community*, trans. M. Hardt. Minneapolis: University of Minnesota Press.

———. (2002). *Remnants of Auschwitz: The witness and the archive.* New York: Zone Books.

Bains, P. (2002). Subjectless subjectivity. In B. Massumi (ed.), *A shock to thought: Expression after Deleuze and Guattari* (pp. 101–116). London and New York: Routledge.

Benjamin, A. (2000). *Architectural philosophy.* London: Althlone Press.

Bullen, E., Robb, S., & Kenway, J. (forthcoming). Creative destruction: Knowledge economy policy and the future of the arts and humanities in the academy. *Journal of Education Policy, 19* (1), 3–22.

Caputo, J. (1993) *Against ethics.* Bloomington: Indiana University Press.

Deleuze, G. (1988). *Foucault,* trans. S. Hand. Minneapolis: University of Minnesota Press.

Deleuze, G. & Guattari, F. (1987). *A thousand plateaus: Capitalism and schizophrenia,* trans. B. Massumi. Minneapolis: University of Minnesota Press.

Guattari, F. (1992). *Chaosmosis: An ethico-aesthetic paradigm,* trans. P. Bains and J. Pefanis. Sydney: Power Publications.

Hardt, M. & Negri, A. (2000). *Empire.* Cambridge: Harvard University Press.

Hartley, J. & Cunningham, S. (2001). Creative industries: From Blue Poles to fat pipes. In Department of Education, Training and Youth Affairs (ed.), *National Humanities and Social Sciences Summit 2001, Position papers* (pp. 16–21). Canberra: Commonwealth of Australia.

Heidegger, M. (1977). *The question concerning technology and other essays,* trans. W. Lovett. New York: Harper & Row.

Heron, K. (1996). From Bauhaus to Koolhaas. *Wired,* 4 July, available online http://www.wired.com/wired/archive/4.07/koolhaas_pr.html (accessed 18 Sept 2002).

Koolhaas, R. (2000). *Mutations.* Barcelona: Actar.

Loo, S. (2002). Dutch courage, Asian know-how: East–West theoretical crossings in contemporary urban studies. In E. Haarhoff, D. Brand, & E. Aitken-Rose (eds.), *Southern Crossings: Proceedings of the Sixth Australasian Urban History/Planning History Conference* (pp. 391–404). Auckland: University of Auckland.

Massumi, B. (2002). *Parables for the virtual: Movement, affect, sensation.* Durham: Duke University Press.

MVRDV (1998). *FARMAX.* Rotterdam: 010 Publishers.

OMA, Koolhaas, R., & Mau, B. (1995). *S, M, L, XL.* Rotterdam: 010 Publishers.

Ruthven, K. (1998). The future of disciplines: A report on ignorance. In Australian Academy of the Humanities (ed.), *Knowing ourselves and others: The humanities in Australia into the 21st century, Vol. 3, Reflective essays* (pp. 95–112). Canberra: Commonwealth of Australia.

Zagala, S. (2002). Aesthetics: A place I've never seen. In B. Massumi (ed.), *A shock to thought: Expression after Deleuze and Guattari* (pp. 20–44). London and New York: Routledge.

*Chika Anyanwu*

---

# INNOVATION AND CREATIVITY
# IN THE HUMANITIES:
# ACCEPTING THE CHALLENGES

There is a saying in Swahili "Mwenzako akinyolewa, tia kichwa chako maji," which means "When you see your neighbour being shaved by force and you are next, you might as well wet your hair so as to make it easy on yourself" (Martin Mhando, personal communication). Is this how the humanities and universities should respond to the knowledge economy and the associated international and national policy imperatives that flow on from it? This is my central question in this chapter. After offering a quick reading of the contemporary scene and of the dominant angst-ridden response of the humanities to it, I make the case that the situation is not as bleak as it first appears. Indeed, I argue that there are current instances of the humanities thriving and that other opportunities for growth exist if the humanities are able to recognize them and to respond creatively. These opportunities draw on the notion that the humanities must partner or perish. I then offer a case study of creative interdisciplinary convergence in the knowledge economy.

## *The Landscape of the Contemporary University*

Universities are losing their centrality as custodians and producers of knowledge in contemporary societies. They are now in competition with other national and international knowledge providers, many of which are cheaper, faster, more flexible, and, some would argue, more closely related to employers' demands and students' needs. For the last two decades of the twentieth century, governments of most political persuasions were almost frenzied in their pursuit of neoliberal marketization and corporatization agendas (Aronowitz, 2000; Readings, 1996). The result has been the rise of what I call corporate democracy. Under corporate democracy, the democratic process is defined by economic power. This is similar to what Bourdieu (1993) sees as production "gate keeping." In a corporate democracy, economic power overwhelms the rights associated with a representative democracy. And further, corporate democracy defines the pursuit of economic self-interest and the achievement of economic self-sufficiency as among the highest "public" goods, and corporate culture as the most suitable culture for public as well as private institutions.

Under these circumstances universities have had their funding slashed and they have also been restructured and re-cultured. For example, Vice Chancellors have become Chief Executive Officers and their public pronouncements now sound like addresses at shareholders' meetings where profit and financial positions are declared to the "stakeholders" and where new strategies for leveraging alternative funding sources for the next fiscal year are enumerated. Also, universities now employ an array of corporate terminology in their daily vocabulary: clients, quality assurance, quality audit, packaging, recruitment drive, strategic initiative and strategic planning, and protecting the economic bottom line. Such terms and the practices associated with them are now commonplace (Strathern, 2000; Jarvis, 2001). Symbolically, the corporate logo has replaced the academic gown. Along with this there has been a shift in the ways in which knowledge is valued. The knowledge that sells is most valued by cash-strapped universities and students now privilege knowledge with a vocational orientation over other knowledges. As Macintyre (this volume) indicates, this has led to the rise and fall of certain fields within the humanities. Demand for such knowledge-enriching courses as philosophy and classics, say, has declined and vocationally oriented courses such as journalism, public relations, film and television, business, and law have become very popular.

Overlaying this broad scenario is the more recent innovation policy agenda that has arisen from the imperatives of the knowledge economy. Innovation has been heavily promoted by the OECD (1999, 2001) and has been taken up in national education and research policies in various ways. Interestingly, within this scenario certain sections of universities have been positioned as important partners with business and industry. In Australia, for example, the *Knowledge and Innovation* policy statement (Kemp, 1999, p. iii) recommended research funding criteria that reward "innovation systems, and research training environments that are responsive to the needs of students and employers."

In 2000 the Innovation Summit implementation final report argued that Australia needs to address the future in an innovative and collaborative manner in order to remain relevant. The foreword to *Innovation: Unlocking the Future* (Commonwealth of Australia, 2000, online) states that there is a need for Australia to "have the right mix of skills and knowledge, strong industries, a robust and flexible economy and most importantly, a culture of innovation." But as Bullen, Robb, and Kenway (2004) demonstrate, the innovation agenda in Australia is primarily oriented towards commerce and is informed by a techno-economic paradigm that implicitly excludes many humanities and creative arts disciplines and explicitly prioritizes science, mathematics, and technology.

This techno-economic inflection of the innovation agenda has provoked considerable disquiet amongst humanities scholars. For instance when the National Humanities and Social Sciences Summit took place in Canberra, Australia in 2001 to consider the effect of these reports on these disciplines, delegates were more anxious than hopeful. At that summit, Malcolm Gillies (2001, p. 47) expressed the fear of many that the innovation agenda would lead to the humanities becoming followers of the science and business disciplines. There is no doubt that the humanities are at risk within such shifting political scenarios. Humanities are one spoke of many in the wheel of change, but a spoke seen by some as broken. When a wheel is in motion a broken spoke can make an annoying clanking noise which can slow down progress but not have the power to stop the wheel's motion. Indeed, when the spoke becomes too annoying it can easily be pulled out completely. This is clearly a fear amongst many humanities scholars.

In contrast, it is my view that we need to reassess our position, to be creative and innovative in addressing what is perceived as a crisis for the humanities and to explore how we might best contribute to the whole new economic paradigm. As Leadbeater (2000, pp. 239–240) says,

> All societies will need to strike a balance between diversity and integration. Creativity stems from the interaction of a diversity of viewpoints, disciplines and outlooks in which ideas are abducted from one area and transplanted to another . . . a fragmented, atomised society without the capacity for collaboration will be creative only spasmodically.

I do not subscribe to Gillies' gloomy scenario for several reasons.

The first and most obvious is the success of the creative industries. This financial success and potential for further growth is documented in Cunningham and in Jeffcutt (this volume). The figures they quote point to the capacity of some sections of the humanities to be innovative in commercial terms, suggesting that at least some of the anxieties felt by humanities scholars are unwarranted. While it is true that the arts and humanities tend to be marginalized in policy, it is the responsibility of the humanities to, among other things, clarify the economic impact of their contributions to governments who understand innovation output primarily in terms of that which can be quantified. Clearly the creative industries provide at least one means by which the humanities can demonstrate their economic contribution. However, this is only part of a much bigger story about the changing nature of the humanities and their broader potential to contribute to an innovation agenda both narrowly defined, as it is currently, and more broadly defined.

The *new* humanities cannot be reduced to traditional disciplines such as philosophy, history, and literature. Neither can their purposes be reduced to such things as critical analysis, the preservation and transmission of tradition, and questioning and maintaining ethical values, as outlined in the introduction to this collection. In the knowledge economy the humanities must embrace both these conventional and important disciplines and traditional roles as well as their role in the creative industries (Caves, 2000; Landry, 2000; Leadbeater, 2000; UK Creative Task Force, 1998) or what Throsby (2001) refers to as the cultural industries.

Gibson, Murphy, and Freestone's (2002) analysis of Throsby's cultural industries includes the core arts industries as well as related industries. Core sectors, according to Gibson et al., include visual and literary arts, live theatre, and music. Others include a mixture of creative and non-creative activities similar to other service and manufacturing industries: printing and publishing, film production and distribution, and photography. These also extend to related sectors like advertising and architectural services (2002, p. 176). A glance at these various subsectors and nontraditional links reveals that the humanities has gone beyond its conventional disciplinary base and has also become intertwined with business and industrial organizational structure. Humanities no longer exist as an independent entity in the academy.

It is possible to argue that if the humanities are not seen as prime movers in the new economy it is partly because broader conceptions of humanities have not kept pace with these changes and that what is now included within the ambit of the *new* humanities is not widely understood. Further, it may not be well or widely understood that, even within technological environments, humanities have important roles to play in, say, ensuring that change adheres to human ethical values and that scientific applications take some cues from historical precedent. Iain McCalman (2001) makes this hybridization process clear when he points out that museums today involve a convergence of arts, technology, and commercial values. Museums are no longer just monuments of antiquity. Kevin Walsh (1992) discusses the widespread revival of interest in heritage and the significant role that heritage is playing in cultural consumption and tourism, effectively competing with other established business ventures. Theme parks like Sea World, Warner Brothers Studios, SciTech, war memorials, and a host of others are examples of the hybridization of art, history and the sciences. The Brisbane Creative Industries' Environmental Scan Audit Report (QUT & Brisbane City, 2002) points out that, in terms of innovation and commercialization, the economic potential of the new humanities compares favorably with any technological or scientific output.

In the new knowledge economy, creativity is the key driver, whereby "knowledge and information are the tools and materials of creativity, innovation, whether in the form of a new technological artefact or new business model or method, is its product" (Florida, 2002, p. 44). Creativity is one of the humanities' strengths and we can harness it properly if we are united. There remains an unhealthy rivalry within the humanities between academics who teach theory and those who teach vocational courses. The collaboration of these two broad positions has the potential to put us at the forefront of innovation and commercialization. Creative thinking is a foundation of the knowledge economy and so is collaborative endeavor, which also contributes to creative thinking. We should realize that the best theory is tested in practice and the best practice is founded on solid theory. "Without creativity we are unable to make full use of the information and experience that is already available to us and is locked up in old structures, old patterns, old concepts and old perceptions" (Edward de Bono, quoted in Cunningham et al., 2003, p. 3). The techno-economic-scientific view of innovation fails to take such matters into account. It does not have a holistic view that recognizes the full potential of all the disciplines or of interdisciplinarity.

Ironically, some of the triggers of such creativity are in the present predicament. Landry (2000, pp. 142–149) identifies some of these creative triggers as: necessity, scarcity, obsolescence, discovery which sometimes is unexpected and unpredictable, luck, ambition and aspiration, competitive pressures, participation in debates, urban visioning, learning from others, inspiration from outside, unexpected connections, and a host of other factors. It is possible to use these "threats" as opportunities. We can do this through collaboration and "coopetition." The metaphor of the spoke in the wheel of change used above implies a collective responsibility and economies of scale.

According to Leadbeater (2000, p. 235), "In 1900 countries were held back by their lack of coal and iron ore. These days the only thing that holds us back is our own inability to make the most of our combined brainpower." For its "combined brain power" to work effectively, humanities academics should consider what Greenleaf (2002) terms "servant leadership" based on a story by Hermann Hesse entitled "Journey to the East." Leo is a servant who sustains the group through his spirit and song. After Leo leaves, the expedition fails. The narrator later finds that Leo is a great spiritual leader. Servant leadership is based on the assumption that change can only occur when a leader produces people who will change. It also implies that human development is a free choice. "The servant leader is servant first" (Greenleaf, 2002, p. 23).

The humanities should see themselves as servant leaders. Their task should be to make themselves indispensable without seeking the limelight. They should act as facilitators in striking a balance between stability and progress, or what Whittle (1997, p. 89) calls the "static quality of immutable principle and the dynamic quality of constant improvement. While the former ensures our safety and security, the latter ensures our progress and learning." The humanities should focus less on being political leaders and more on ways of interacting with others to build a sustainable society. Human development is less influenced by significant events than the daily "interaction between our choice of adaptive mechanisms and our sustained relationships with other people" (Vaillant, 1977, p. 368).

## Creative Convergence in the Knowledge Economy

Let me now offer two examples of creative interdisciplinarity across the humanities–sciences divide: the cross-disciplinary research group, the Convergent Communications Research Group (CCRG), formed in 2002 at the University of Adelaide, and the newly established Bachelor of Media Program at the same university. Both examples demonstrate how the humanities can become innovative by forging collaborative partnerships with other disciplines and fields within and beyond the university environment.

The CCRG brings together "disparate disciplines plug[ged] into digital media" (Illing, 2002, p. 48). It is a convergence of professionals from engineering, economics, law, industry, telecommunications, and humanities. The group is located in the School of Engineering. It consults, carries out research, and makes submissions to governments and industry in areas in which its members have expertise. Despite the disparate professional backgrounds of its members, many of its projects are jointly executed. The principle of the group is collaboration, irrespective of the specialist focus of the research project. The group philosophy is that everybody has a role to play in any activity that impacts on society. This stance does not involve a simplistic approach to issues, but challenges every member's specialist skills in aligning to a common goal. In every domain of existence there are leaders and collaborators. In the same vein every project carried out by the CCRG identifies its leadership through task specialization requirements.

Take the example of a recent tender submission by the CCRG to the NOIE (National Office for Information Economy, Australia) on "the implications of the emergence of broadband distribution mediums for the production of digital content and applications." The tender process involved the pattern of collaboration outlined above. Every member researched different aspects of the project and the final draft of the application was vetted at a brainstorming session where each discipline specialist's representation was critiqued before the tender document was completed. All submissions are made under the CCRG umbrella, not under the name of the individual member who may have initiated or been awarded the project, or even under the discipline from which that member may come. This structure does not prevent the member from claiming equivalent research performance points from such an activity within his or her department. Such a member will claim a fractional percentage of the total research point based on the number of members involved in a particular project.

The group holds a monthly breakfast meeting where new ideas and new opportunities for research funding are brainstormed or updated. At the end of each session, members nominate projects or aspects of projects that they would like to carry out. A deadline is then set for members to "report." A ratification date is set when all the reports will be evaluated against the selected project's brief. At this meeting every report is scrutinized to ensure that it conforms to the client's expectations. A member who has technical and other expertise in the field of inquiry then edits the final tender document to ensure that it conforms to its relevant industry expectations.

A project on a 3G mobile [cellular] phone, for example, will logically be located within telecommunications engineering, but its applications from a consumer perspective or litigious social consequence or cost implications will cut across humanities, law, and economics respectively. Another example can be drawn from the group's current application to the Australian Research Council for an Industry-Linkage grant to enable a study of the creative industries in South Australia. This project aligns mainly with the humanities, but its execution will cut across all the other disciplines in the research group. Our intellectual capital in the group harnesses our differences to enrich our output.

The CCRG can be described a "creative milieu," using Landry's (2000, p. 133) definition:

> A creative milieu is either a cluster or part of a city . . . that contains the necessary preconditions in terms of hard and soft infrastructure to generate a flow of ideas and inventions. Such a milieu is a physical setting where a critical mass of entrepreneurs, intellectuals, social activists, artists, administrators, power brokers or

students can operate in an open-minded, cosmopolitan context and where face to face interaction creates new ideas, artefacts, products, services and institutions and as a consequence contributes to economic success.

The CCRG is also a clearinghouse of ideas. Ideas are generated individually and collectively. Within this seemly loose formation lies a tight ideological formation, a collaborative spirit that overcomes all members' shortfalls in research input and output. The chances of attracting research grants and of generating research output are considerably enhanced for individual researchers because they are members of a collective. Members use each other as sources of critical evaluation during brainstorming sessions.

The philosophy behind this strategy is that submissions made to any organization or government should address the concerns of cross-sections of society and take into account diverse societal opinions. While the engineer brings a certain technical rigor; the lawyer looks at legal implications; the economist evaluates economic and financial implications; while the humanities expert evaluates socio-cultural implications. The CCRG philosophy and strategy resonates with the idea of the knowledge economy as a convergence economy, an economy of collective social responsibility. As Landry (2000, p. 139) puts it, "In the urban context creativity and innovation need to be seen as an holistic, integrated process covering every aspect of urban life from the economic, political, cultural, environmental and social-multiple innovativeness. Only then can the city deal with the strains and distresses of global transformations and remain efficient and effective."

The Bachelor of Media is a program that was set up in a similar collaborative spirit. It is an interdisciplinary degree within the Faculty of Humanities and Social Sciences, University of Adelaide. It cuts across many faculties within the university as well as industry. Its success and strength stems from its ability to forge professional relationships with disciplines outside its traditional humanities enclave. For example its radio broadcast production specialization is jointly designed and taught with Radio Adelaide; the television and interactive video production specialization is currently being designed in collaboration with the Australian Broadcasting Commission and Adelaide Institute of TAFE (Technical and Further Education); the indigenous media specialization is jointly designed and taught with the Centre for Aboriginal Studies and with indigenous elders; the multimedia specialization is taught in collaboration with the Schools of Engineering and Architecture; the creative writing and publishing specialization is jointly taught with the Department of English; while media management, marketing, and electronic commerce specializations are jointly taught with the School of Commerce. Students are exposed to a variety of professional areas of specialization, which prepares them for the challenges of future employment and opens up a new paradigm in academic collaboration.

On their own, each of the above specializations may not command enough critical mass to attract any strategic investment in their establishment. Collaboratively, however, each of the contributing faculties and disciplines is able to utilize its existing resources to deliver programs that serve students' needs and industry expectations without compromising quality, at the same time generating enough income to sustain the program. Under the old school structure of the university, the questions and problems would include: "Who owns the degree? Who gets the teaching load and who pays for staffing and resources? What constitutes humanities components in the program?" But in this program we look at degrees and awards as products of collective responsibility. They arise in part at least from students' cross-disciplinary intellectual engagements during the course of their study.

In the new knowledge economy the humanities are part of a new economic forge. "Scientific and artistic endeavor, for instance, have become industries unto themselves, and they have combined in new ways to create still newer industries. The joint expansion of technological innovation and creative content work has increasingly become the motor force of economic growth" (Florida, 2002, p. 44). The philosophy behind the collaborative structure of the media program is that media is at the center of every current activity. It has an intrusive connectivity which does not discriminate between disciplines or fields. It is part of every sphere of modern endeavor; therefore any study of the media should reflect these interdisciplinary connections.

A further reason for this collaboration is that there are many students who prefer to study humanities courses, but who end up in other disciplines because of job insecurity caused by changes in the global employment market as well as by shifts in government funding policies. In order to retain such students in humanities programs we must be innovative in either designing courses with high employment prospects or in collaborating with other disciplines that have new job market oriented courses. As long as we continue to think that the global economy must support the humanities without adapting to its changes, our prospective students will go elsewhere. We need to have answers when students ask, "What are the job prospects associated with this degree?" With a collaborative spirit we will be in a better position to design programs that appeal to students and to enhance their job prospects whilst also instilling the critical skills and socio-cultural sensibilities for which the humanities are known. At the core of this interdisciplinary collaboration within the media program lies a strong emphasis on critical thinking and analysis. While students are equipped and empowered with these core humanities values, they are also exposed to the methodological and empirical reasoning of social sciences and commerce. In their final year of study they carry out a project that aligns their critical skills with their vocational area of specialization.

## Conclusion

*Our deepest fear is not that we are inadequate.*
*Our deepest fear is that we are powerful beyond measure.*
*It is our light, not our darkness, that most frightens us.*
*We ask ourselves, who am I to be brilliant, gorgeous, talented and fabulous?*
*Actually, who are you not to be?*
*. . . Your playing small doesn't serve the world.*
*There's nothing enlightened about shrinking so that other people*
*won't feel insecure around you.*
(WILLIAMSON, 1992, PP. 190–191)

This extract from Williamson's *A Return to Love* summarizes the potential within humanities. We need to let the world see what we can offer and not just focus on what governments can do for the humanities. Neither should they be relegated to the status of cultural archivists or arbiters of the social conscience. A key to the future of the humanities in the knowledge economy resides in a collaborative alliance between the humanities broadly defined (the "old" and the "new") and other disciplines. None should be seen as a half brother or sister to the other. Rather we should look at collaborative ventures from a Gestaltian perspective which says that the whole is greater that the sum of its component parts. Collaboration or "coopetition" is the key word in the knowledge economy.

## References

Aronowitz, S. (2000). *The knowledge factory: Dismantling the corporate university and creating true higher learning*. Boston, MA: Beacon Press.

Bourdieu, P. (1993). *The field of cultural production*. Cambridge: Polity Press.

Bullen, E., Robb, S., & Kenway, J. (2004). "Creative destruction": Knowledge economy policy and the future of the arts and humanities in the academy. *Journal of Education Policy, 19* (1) 3–22.

Caves, R. (2000). *Creative industries*. Massachusetts: Harvard University Press.

Commonwealth of Australia (2000). *Innovation: Unlocking the future: Final report of the Innovation Summit Implementation Group*. Canberra: Commonwealth of Australia.

Cunningham, S., Hearn, G., Cox, S., Ninan, A., & Keane, M. (2003). *Brisbane's creative industries 2003*. Report delivered to Brisbane City Council, Community and Economic Development. Brisbane: Creative Industries Research and Applications Centre, Queensland University of Technology.

Florida, R. (2002). *The rise of the creative class: And how it's transforming work, leisure, community and everyday life*. New York: Basic Books.

Gibson, C., Murphy, P., & Freestone, R. (2002). Employment and socio-spatial relations in Australia's cultural economy. *Australian Geographer, 33* (2), 173–189.

Gillies, M. (2001). Commercialisation and globalisation. In Department of Education, Training and Youth Affairs (ed.), *National Humanities and Social Sciences Summit, 2001, Position papers* (pp. 41–48). Canberra: Commonwealth of Australia.

Illing, D. (2002). Disparate disciplines plug into digital media. *The Australian*, 16 October, p. 48.

Jarvis, P. (2001). *Universities and corporate universities: The higher learning industry in global society*. London: Kogan Page.

Kemp, D. (1999). *Knowledge and innovation: A policy statement on research and research training*. Canberra: Commonwealth of Australia.

Landry, C. (2000). *The creative city: A toolkit for urban innovators*. London: Earthscan.

Leadbeater, C. (2000). *Living on thin air: The new economy*. London: Penguin.

McCalman, I. (2001). Museum and heritage management in the new economy. In Department of Education, Training and Youth Affairs (ed.), *National Humanities and Social Sciences Summit, 2001, Position papers* (pp. 11–21). Canberra: Commonwealth of Australia.

OECD (Organization for Economic Cooperation and Development) (1999). *Managing national innovation systems*. Paris: OECD.

———. (2001). *Innovative clusters: Drivers of national innovation systems*. Paris: OECD.

Queensland University of Technology (QUT) & Brisbane City (2002). Brisbane's creative industries 2002: An interim snapshot environmental scan audit. Brisbane: QUT.

Readings, B. (1996). *The university in ruins*. Cambridge, MA: Harvard University Press.

Strathern, M. (2000). *Audit cultures: Anthropological studies in accountability, ethics and the academy*. London and New York: Routledge/Falmer.

Throsby, D. (2001). Defining the artistic workforce: The Australian experience. *Poetics, 28*, 255–271.

Vaillant, G.E. (1977). *Adaptation to life*. Boston: Little Brown.

Walsh, K. (1992). *The representation of the past: Museums and heritage in the post-modern world*. London: Routledge.

Whittle, D. (1997). *Cyberspace: The human dimension*. New York: W.H. Freeman and Company.

Williamson, M. (1992). *A return to love: Reflections on the principles of "A course in miracles."* New York: Harper Collins. N.B.: This is often found on the Internet incorrectly stated to be a quotation by Nelson Mandela from his Inauguration Speech in 1994, available online http://www.skdesigns.com/internet/articles/quotes/williamson.html (accessed August 2003).

## ·8·

*Susan Luckman*

---

# MORE THAN THE SUM
# OF ITS PARTS: THE HUMANITIES
# AND COMMUNICATING THE
# "HIDDEN WORK" OF RESEARCH

Informed as it is by ethnographic as well as critical/textual approaches, and engaged as it is with the quotidian and popular culture, cultural studies has been relatively successful within the humanities in securing competitive research funding. Its potential to engage in "laboratory-style" research—that is, research with clearly defined, comprehensible, qualitative and quantitative methodologies and neatly demarcated research outcomes—means that aspects of cultural studies as an interdisciplinary (anti)discipline have been well-placed to engage in the sort of consultancy cultural policy style research being encouraged in the contemporary funding milieu where clear, preferably economically viable, outcomes are desired. In spite of this the extent to which cultural studies, like other humanities disciplines, has had to reconceptualize its project away from pure and/or curiousity-driven research remains a point of great contention and concern within the field.

This chapter will examine this tension through the lens of research in Australia into contemporary youth music cultures. In so doing, it will consider what positive and valuable lessons can be learnt as a result of the push to force humanities practitioners to think more in terms of the wider social value of their (still largely publicly funded) work. However, whilst focusing on youth subcultures, a popular object of study for cultural studies scholars since the early days of the Birmingham Centre for Contemporary Cultural Studies in the 1970s, I will also argue that an emphasis on cultural policy or "creative industries" style directed research engagements are only one part of the wider humanities research culture that needs ongoing support. The reasons for this are two-fold.

Firstly, and simply, much valuable humanities work simply cannot be done within such a research model promoted in knowledge economy policy; literary criticism, philosophy, art history, among other disciplines, remain dominated by research practices that by necessity tend to be solitary and disengaged from collaboration with government or industry. Secondly, and given my own location as a cultural studies scholar this is the point I wish to develop in greatest detail here, even where it is possible and desirable, the pragmatically engaged work being undertaken within the community and in conjunction with various research partners which is being offered up by some stakeholders as the way forward for the humanities, is not possible without a strong history of so-called "pure" research upon which it can draw. Consequently, without a strong, broad, and innovative research base, the ongoing viability of even these more transparently instrumental facets of humanities scholarship is at stake. Underpinning my overall argument is a belief that the humanities play, and must continue to play, an invaluable role in society and culture.

## "Throwing the Baby Out with the Bath Water," or, the "Hidden Work" of the Humanities

Following on from the work of medical sociologist Anselm Strauss, Susan Leigh Starr (1991) employs the idea of "hidden work" as a means by which to account for what economist Paul David refers to as the "productivity paradox" of information technology. That is why it is that in many firms and even at the level of national economies the introduction of information technology has led to a decline in productivity (Starr, 1991). As Starr and David point out, the answer to this question lies in the simple fact that the introduction of new systems precipitates the need for a myriad of intangible changes, and hence leads to costs that are virtually impossible to measure using standard economic analyses. This is especially the case in regard to the "hidden work" employees undertake to keep systems working and operating. Such work is not just product-oriented, but consists of activities such as emotional support and community building.

Taking the workplace as a social system whose lessons can legitimately be mapped onto larger social systems—society as a civil, social, and cultural whole itself, for example—the "productivity paradox" furnishes us with a "way in" on debates about the valuable role the arts and humanities have to play in redressing societal imbalances that prioritize the economic at the expense of social and cultural needs, in what Ulrich Beck (1992) refers to as the "risk society." For example, in an age where we are theoretically "all more connected than ever before," it provides a means by which to examine rising levels of anxiety, stress, depression, loneliness, social dislocation, and uncertainty. It may also provide a way to examine the rise of extremism and the targeting of easily identifiable scapegoats, a trend particularly evident in debates around immigration and the threat of terrorism in Europe, the United States, and Australia. Similarly, access to more information through immersion in the "knowledge economy" does not intrinsically make us better or smarter citizens and employees, especially when much of that information is of dubious quality and few of us have the time to engage in more than a superficial examination of its relative merits. Furthermore, in an increasingly flexible and mobile world where traditional social institutions such as the family are evolving, it is essential that the valuable and legitimate role played by new forms of affinity and community are recognized, supported, and encouraged. Research in the "soft sciences" is not just in a uniquely valuable position to identify the specifics of the "productivity paradox" of contemporary society, but to come up with creative and innovative responses to fundamental human questions and problems.

Returning again to Strauss, while the more specifically interpersonal activity of providing "emotional support" may not be self-evidently mappable onto humanities' engagement with the small "c" commonwealth, I would argue that the sorts of critical literacies, heightened social awareness, historical context, and communication skills students of the arts and humanities take with them throughout their lives makes an invaluable contribution to the emotional maturity of all contemporary societies. In regard to the more specific question of higher education funding, the research we undertake, in all its myriad forms, has long been relied upon to inform this teaching, and directly allows for the ongoing viability of innovative research itself. With its emphasis upon research as an entrepreneurial activity leading to neatly and clearly identifiable commercial outcomes in the forms of products, services, and businesses, knowledge economy policies risk overlooking the role arts and humanities-based research plays in maintaining socially and politically sustainable societies.

Additionally, we also need to think in terms of the sustainability of the higher education system itself and the "hidden work" required to maintain it in the new knowledge-based economy. All universities need to preserve their reputation for scholarship if they are to be competitive in the global education market, a market that in Australia, the third largest exporter of higher education after the United States and United Kingdom, earns more in export dollars than the wool industry and as much as wheat. As columnist Ross Fitzgerald (2003) comments, under-funded higher education systems cannot sustain such phenomenal growth indefinitely. Universities in this global economy are only as good and hence as profitable as their reputations. As strains in the form of plagiarism allegations and anxiety over whistleblowers coming clean on purported incidences of "soft marking" and research fraud attest, the system is beginning to show signs of crumbling under the pressure. Or, as Fitzgerald phrases it in a fashion that parallels my own arguments vis-à-vis subcultural studies' lessons for sustainability in the humanities: "we are rapidly selling off the family silver" (2003, p. 13).

*Cultural Policy: Positive Lessons to Be Learned*

So how might we best begin to identify and communicate clearly the "hidden work" we do? As already mentioned, one of the more obvious places this has been done is in the area of cultural policy, especially as it relates to the arts and media industries. Engaged as it is in a process of collaborative work, cultural policy-style research inherently seeks to include constituencies beyond the academy as research partners, stakeholders, and audience. The process of widening out our audience in these instances is quite frequently aided by the grounded nature of the research; that is, the specific explication of a tangible organization or field, and therefore the relative ease of translating research outcomes into media-friendly information chunks and effective policy initiatives.

In recent years, studies undertaken on the value of maintaining and supporting local live music venues in the face of gentrification and initially successful calls for establishments to be closed down following noise complaints, are important examples of this kind of community collaboration (see for instance Flew et al., 2001; Johnson & Homan, 2002). For example, *Music Industry Development and Brisbane's Future as a Creative City* (Flew et al., 2001), a report undertaken by researchers from the Creative Industries Faculty of the Queensland University of Technology (QUT) and funded by the Brisbane City Council, notes that, although the contemporary local music scene has its origins "in an oppositional subculture that existed in the city in the 1970s and 1980s,"

> Understanding music as a creative industry, this project found that contemporary popular music is central to Brisbane's cultural identity as a creative city. . . . Music is central to the "night-time economy" of the city, and attendance at live music venues provides valuable economic spin-offs to the leisure, hospitality, entertainment and tourism industries. Music is also an important industry in its own right, being a major item of cultural consumption, and is experiencing growth at regional, national and international levels. (Flew et al., 2001, p. 7)

However, success within such cultural industries does not happen over-night, is never guaranteed, does not occur in a vacuum, and, significantly, it is rarely successfully imposed from above. In order for a scene to germinate, a diverse cultural mix of knowledges, networks, and resources is required. To this end, the report calls for government support of this "soft infrastruc-ture" in the form not of direct governmental support, but rather through the avoidance of government policies that hinder the industry's develop-ment "such as inappropriate application of planning, zoning and noise abatement regulations" (Flew et al., 2001, p. 8). This, the report argues, is all the more necessary as "top down" attempts to just "pick winners" and support them to the detriment of the wider scene are not ultimately to the benefit of this important cultural industry The report gathered data to sup-port the qualitatively championed point that diversity needs to be main-tained as a key generator of innovation. In this instance it identified the need for a healthy, grassroots "soft infrastructure" to be continually feed-ing—"bottom-up"—a healthy music industry, and night-time economy generally. Such a scenario can metaphorically be applied to the humanities themselves.

What this report, my own research into contemporary dance music cul-tures in Australia, and a vast array of other research examining grassroots youth practices demonstrates is that diverse oppositional and/or alternative expressive scenes are an essential part of not just the democratic process but consumer capitalism itself (ask any trend spotter or "cool hunter"). They are, however, under threat from this very force. Media proliferation and the ubiq-uitous presence of ICTs (information and communication technologies) places those working in the creative industries under increasing pressure to deliver novel products and services ever more quickly than before, with the effect that the gap between the underground and mainstream is becoming ex-tremely weak. As a result there exists a creeping anxiety now that nothing is actually new anymore. Is consumer capitalism "eating itself" and could the same potentially be true for the humanities?

*Academic Sustainability and the "Hidden Work" of Pure Research:*
*The Limits of Cultural Policy and Consultancy as a "Magical Solution"*
*to Humanities Research Funding*

In a passage from William Gibson's *All Tomorrow's Parties* (1999) two cyber-punks engage in a dialogue in which they lament the death of subculture fol-lowing capitalist "over-farming":

"It's what we do now instead of bohemias," he says.

"Instead of what?"

"Bohemias. Alternative subcultures. They were a crucial aspect of industrial civilization in the two previous centuries. They were where industrial civilization went to dream. A sort of unconscious R&D, exploring alternate societal strategies. Each one would have a dress code, characteristic forms of artistic expression, a substance or substances of choice, and a set of sexual values at odds with those of the culture at large. And they did, frequently, have locales with which they became associated. But they became extinct."

"Extinct?"

"We started picking them before they could ripen." (p. 174)

Innovation, originality, the "next big thing" do not materialize out of thin air under pressure. Forty years of research into youth subcultures have shown us that such subculture scenes are the R&D (research and development) parks of media, fashion, and allied creative industries. Maintenance of diversity, the "unpopular," the marginal, the not economically obvious, is an essential component not just of democratic health (see also Potter, this volume). Without a broad base from which ideas can rise, consumer capitalism would itself be unsustainable as an ongoing purveyor of the novel. It is a sad fact that governments and the mass media amongst others need to be constantly reminded of this. Just as a healthy local music industry cannot be fabricated from scratch through the top-down impetus of government, so too do the humanities need to be given space to nurture the new and organically evolve. This necessitates support for the sorts of work that are traditionally undertaken outside of economic paradigms. It necessitates a recognition that "difficult" humanities research informs more palatable research outcomes such as the consultancy-style studies being undertaken around cultural industries.

In this regard at least, the base lessons learnt from over thirty years of cultural studies' theoretical work into youth subcultures can be drawn upon to further illuminate this dilemma. Despite later recantations or development of their ideas, the original Birmingham "canon" consists of a diverse series of texts released over a number of years, and three in particular stand out as the specific texts that set up the Birmingham Centre for Cultural Studies' "textual" model: Phil Cohen's "Subcultural conflict and working-class community" (1981 [1972]), Dick Hebdige's *Subculture: The Meaning of Style* (1991 [1979]), and the anthology *Resistance Through Rituals: Youth Subcultures in Post-War Britain* (Hall & Jefferson, 1976). These studies have provided a point of reference for almost thirty years of subsequent subcultural study, for it was in these discussions that a number of the center's key tropes were elaborated. In this body of work, subcultural participation was identified as an explicitly working-class phenomenon; one that offered the young dispossessed a "magical solution" to the contradictions of their lived, class-bound experience. Examining subcultures from within a Marxist framework, scholars at the center used the Gramscian concept of hegemony as a way of understanding subcultural practice, to use Hebdige's words, as a kind of "semiotic guerrilla warfare" (1991, p. 105).

At a local level it is tempting to suggest that industry or community linkage-style projects are being used by Australian humanities scholars to build "hidden" spaces for the conduct of "pure" research. But this too reinforces the short-term and sees the situation in far too narrow terms. What, rather, we need to do is to be unafraid to (re)make the case that universities, like subcultures, are key generators of innovation, but innovation that cannot necessarily be performed on demand. Nor is it necessarily best capitalized upon by those whose expertise lies in generating these knowledges. The writing is clearly on the wall around OECD nations, and researchers do increasingly need to be located within wider collaborative networks of skill and expertise.

While the sort of partnerships that have been actively sought by practitioners in the area of cultural policy provide a model for the sorts of grounded community-centered outcomes humanities research can facilitate, the sorts of issues and audiences being addressed need to be wider if the humanities are not to become a consultancy arm of the government of the day. Further, such research needs to be funded alongside more "pure" research, not wholly subsume it.

In many ways this is not a new argument. As Cunningham noted in a judicious engagement with criticism of cultural policy's "handmaiden" role,

> From where does tomorrow's public debate and potential consensus issue? From today's utopian, left-of-field thinking that, at the time of its formulation, might appear counterindicated by the realities of the public world. The clearest example of this is the sourcing of "femocrat" reformism by feminist movement politics, as an especially developed phenomenon in Australia . . . Similar relationships hold between the environmental movement and green politics, or between ethnic advocacy and official discourses of multiculturalism. (1992, pp. 9–10)

But in this age of creative industries and an emphasis on "content," we need to look anew at content generation and look more seriously to protect and maintain all those engines actually driving content innovation in an age of vociferous "idea over-farming" (be it consumer product or, less tangibly, new knowledges). As subcultural studies and wider music industries inform us, these drivers of innovation lie in broad-based "soft infrastructures," for after all there are only so many top-down "manufactured" music artists or so much faux rebellion the market can, and wants to, absorb.

## *Conclusion*

National and supranational knowledge economy policy enunciations clearly signal a threat to the ongoing feasibility of the arts and humanities. Further partnerships in this area need to be pursued in balance with "pure" research, rather than pandering to economically motivated governmental desires to do away with scholarship with more medium- to long-term outcomes, such as providing the theoretical models that allow us to make sense of "real world" case studies or that give rise to challenging new artistic works. Such a call need not be as radical nor old school as it might *prima facie* appear. Already limited recognition for this case is emerging from within some policy circles. For example, Charles Leadbeater, a key advisor whose thoughts on the new economy and the "third way" have been highly influential in the current British government's approach to knowledge generation, creative industries, and entrepreneurship, contends that "Universities should be the open-cast mines of the knowledge economy" (2000, p. 114). Even more palpably, he calls for the wider adoption of the classic critical role of the humanities beyond their traditional home as a key basis for success in the twenty-first century: "Knowledge entrepreneurship will only thrive within regions and companies with a culture of dissent, dispute, disrespect for authority, diversity and experimentation" (Leadbeater, 2000, p. 107). Yet, in Australia, it is this very space and basis of success that is most under threat within the humanities, as we are asked to recast our research emphasis in terms of greater links with external, often commercial or governmental, stakeholders who may well be reluctant to pay for a critique that disputes the foundation of their practices.

## *References*

Beck, U. (1992). *The risk society: Towards a new modernity*, trans. M. Ritter. London: Sage.

Cohen, P. (1981). Subcultural conflict and working-class community. In D. Hobson, S. Hall, A. Lowe, & P. Willis (eds.), *Culture, media, language: Working papers in cultural studies, 1972–79* (pp. 78–87). London: Hutchinson in association with the Centre for Contemporary Cultural Studies, University of Birmingham.

Cunningham, S. (1992). *Framing culture: Criticism and policy in Australia*. North Sydney: Allen & Unwin.

Fitzgerald, R. (2003). We're starving a nice little earner. *The Australian*, 11 September, p. 13.

Flew, T., Ching, G., Stafford, A., & Tacchi, J. (2001). *Music industry development and Brisbane's future as a creative city*. Brisbane: Brisbane City Council and Creative Industries Research and Applications Centre (CIRAC), Queensland University of Technology.

Gibson, W. (1999). *All tomorrow's parties*. London: Viking.

Hall, S. & Jefferson, T. (ed.) (1976) *Resistance through rituals: Youth subcultures in post-war Britain*. London: Hutchinson & Co.

Hebdige, D. (1991). *Subculture: The meaning of style*. London and New York: Routledge.

Johnson, B. & Homan, S. (2002). *Vanishing acts: An inquiry into the state of live popular music opportunities in New South Wales*. Sydney: Australia Council and the NSW Ministry for the Arts.

Leadbeater, C. (2000). *Living on thin air: The new economy*. London: Penguin.

Starr, S.L. (1991). The sociology of the invisible: The primacy of work in the writings of Anselm Strauss. In D.R. Maines (ed.), *Social organization and social process: Essays in honor of Anselm Strauss* (pp. 265–284). New York: Aldine De Gruyter.

# · 9 ·

*Sarah Redshaw*

---

# THE USES OF KNOWLEDGE: COLLABORATION, COMMERCIALIZATION, AND THE DRIVING CULTURES PROJECT

Higher education and research will play a pivotal role in the transition of advanced economies into knowledge economies, and they will contribute in three key ways: knowledge production (development and provision of new knowledge); knowledge transmission (education and development of human capital); and knowledge transfer (dissemination of knowledge and input to problem solving) (OECD, 1996, p. 21). They will further contribute to the growth of the knowledge economy through participation in knowledge networks and national systems of innovation, that is, through collaboration with industry and government. As part of national systems of innovation, higher education and research are no longer the responsibility of separate specialist portfolios. Instead, they are increasingly subject to the interventions of "whole-of-government" policy approaches (for example, Canada, Australia, U.K., and New Zealand) and the subject of recommendations from international and supranational organizations (for example, European Commission, World Bank, and OECD). According to the OECD (2002, p. 55), for instance, governments take a role as catalysts and organizers, among other things,

> Structuring the innovation process by: enhancing firms' innovative capacities; exploiting the power of the market; securing investment in knowledge; promoting

the commercialization of publicly-funded research; promoting cluster development; promoting internationally-open networks. (OECD, 2002, p. 55)

The problem for the arts and humanities is that when supranational organizations like the OECD talk about national systems of innovation, knowledge production, transmission and transfer, and knowledge networks, they are referring principally to science systems and this translates into the policy and funding priorities at the level of the nation-state.

As a result, the question of how higher education and research in the arts and humanities should evolve for a knowledge economy is vexed. On the one hand, the dominant science and techno-economic paradigm informing the knowledge economy has led to a perception among policy makers that the capacity of the humanities to contribute to the knowledge economy is minimal at best (Bullen, Robb, & Kenway, 2004). As a consequence, they are frequently marginalized in policy (see Cunningham, this volume). On the other hand, humanities scholars are not only inclined to this same misperception, they are frequently resistant to knowledge economy imperatives to collaborate with industry and to find commercial applications for research. This resistance is understandable, but problematic, and not only because of the impediment it creates to the necessary evolution of the arts and humanities. It is also conceptually problematic, and often informed by reductive notions of the economy and, in short, fears about the uses of knowledge.

This chapter seeks to address some of these concerns and to achieve two things: to show that the humanities can contribute to the knowledge economy and to show that it can do so without inevitably compromising the distinctive qualities and benefits of arts and humanities education and research. To do this, this chapter takes the example of a successful cultural studies research project that explores the cultures of driving and their influence on young drivers.

### The Uses of Knowledge

*Even though cultural studies that looks at popular culture has the power to move intellectuals both out of the academy and into the streets where our work can be shared with a larger audience, many critical thinkers who do cultural criticism are afraid to make that move.*
(HOOKS, 1994, P. 4)

What is important in bell hooks' statement is the idea of sharing knowledge—our work—with larger audiences, and the reluctance of academics, even cultural studies academics, to make that move. Universities face enormous challenges at the moment. The knowledge economy is changing our ideas about the role of the university in knowledge creation. With increasing numbers of university graduates in the workforce, knowledge is being produced at a range of different sites, mostly beyond the confines of the university (Gibbons et al., 1994). The emphasis is increasingly on applied knowledge, not only in terms of commercial application, but in terms of an engagement with social and community concerns.

In this context, the defense of traditional academic values limits the future possibilities for humanities research and education. "Liberal" values uphold an idea of the university that emerged during the Enlightenment, values extensively and persuasively challenged by philosophers, feminists, sociologists, and cultural studies and politics scholars from within the academy (see, for example, Bordo, 1987; Connolly, 1991, 1995; Mohanty, 2002). Feminists within philosophy, for instance, have critiqued philosophy's abstraction and remoteness from everyday issues, arguing for a more concrete engagement with moral, political, and social issues (Benhabib & Cornell, 1987; Lloyd & Gatens, 1999). Liberal and Enlightenment thought privileges the analytical and universal capacities of reason, which is distanced from its particular social and experiential contexts. Impersonal, disembodied, abstract, and universalizing, reason is related to the liberal idea of the individual as separate and independent, rather than interdependent.

The distinction between pure and applied knowledge that Enlightenment thought cultivated has been durable and it continues to inform the way in which the role of the university and its disciplines is conceptualized. It also provides a paradigmatic frame for understanding and interpreting the impact of knowledge economy policy on the humanities. Cooper, Hinkson and Sharp (2002), for example, claim that applied and vocational disciplines are flourishing at the expense of "traditional knowledge" and that the university is being undermined by the privileging of the instrumental over the cultural-interpretive. Rehearsing Gaita's (2002) argument, Cooper et al. (2002) emphasize the role of the university as an institution that needs to somehow stand outside the world of utilitarianism. Contextualization, accountability, the massification of higher education, and the requirement to generate income via industry collaboration are perceived as threats to "truth," "freedom of thought," and "pure knowledge." Readings (1996) and Coady (2000) both appeal to the idea of a university based on the Enlightenment. Coady (1998) argues that liberal concepts of anti-relativism, traditional values of "truth," and the intrinsic value of the pure disciplines are being obliterated by vocational education.

In contrast to the emphasis on Enlightenment notions of truth, Gibbons (1994), Gibbons et al., 1994), and Nowotny, Scott, and Gibbons (2002) reconceptualize the importance of academic research and truth values in terms of social relevance:

> To suggest that reliable knowledge must engage the social world more openly and directly is not to seek to diminish but to enhance its status and validity, by arguing that reliable knowledge—to remain reliable—has also to be socially robust knowledge. (Nowotny et al., 2002, p. 178)

Socially robust knowledge is relational, rather than relative; allowed to evolve, it can become stable; it is prospective, that is, capable of dealing with unknown and unforeseeable contexts; and it is strongly empirical in the sense that it is "subject to frequent testing, feedback and improvement, because it is open-ended" (Nowotny et al., 2002, p. 167). The robustness results from the infiltration and improvement of knowledge by social knowledge.

If we are to take better and more explicit account of the social, we need to reconceptualize the way in which academe contributes to knowledge creation, in ways that are unlike those inscribed in traditional academic values. In terms of the humanities, this may mean more interdisciplinary collaboration and developing a capacity to link with our counterparts in science and technology. It may mean that less of our research is curiosity-driven, and more is focused on outcomes of national significance. It may mean accepting that some of our research will have commercial applications within the public and private sectors. The use of ideas and their commercial value are linked. We can frame this relationship in terms of instrumentality or economic gain, or we can frame it in terms of social responsiveness to community concerns.

### Driving Cultures: The Project

Driving Cultures and a series of related projects investigating driver behavior are founded on the premise that driving has a culture through which attitudes, beliefs, and expectations about driving are constructed and maintained. The research community[1] that developed the projects emphasizes community connectivity and the importance of the contribution of different voices not overwhelmed by theory. The Driving Cultures projects are based on a community inquiry approach to problem solving which seeks to elicit and engage with the knowledge of different stakeholders and interest groups. The young people involved in these projects are not the subjects of the research; rather, they are participants in knowledge production.

Driving Cultures examines the meanings young people generate about driving behaviors, cars, road rules, and traffic. It emphasizes that, in addition to the usual car handling skills, approaches to educating young and inexperienced drivers need to include other skills related to driving. They need to acknowledge that some of the unsafe practices of young drivers are directly influenced by similar driving practices in the wider community. Conventional research into driver behavior designed to reduce the risk of injury and road accident fatalities is typically conducted by psychologists or engineers and tends to rely on quantitative research methods. Driver behavior is currently being evaluated using a cognitive approach that focuses on the individual (Parker, Manstead, & Stradling, 1995; Parker, West, Stradling, & Manstead, 1995), rather than on members of a driving culture or community.

Likewise, the project offers an approach to driver education that disrupts conventional road safety pedagogies. The traditional approach is to present statistics and graphic pictures in a lecture-style format with the opportunity for questions at the end of the session. In contrast, the Driving Cultures approach is more consultative and discussion-focused. Young drivers talk about their views, issues, opinions, and experiences related to driving in a guided discussion. They are provided with an opportunity to reflect on driving practice, their own as well as the driving practices of others. The reflexivity or critical awareness and understanding of research practices, cultural forms and structures, and social processes that the project promotes are of course the key work of the humanities.

Driving Cultures draws on cultural studies, social psychology, philosophy, and social studies of technology, and utilizes semiotic analysis. This involves reflection on the representation of driving and driving cultures in twentieth-century literature, film, and television commercials. It also provides an opportunity to evaluate the appeal of commercial advertising and public road safety campaigns. It is likely that the project will develop educational programs based on semiotic analysis of car advertisements and film scenes. By confronting and evaluating the cultural values that advertising exploits and reinforces, students are better able to make choices about how they relate to and recreate driving cultures.

The Driving Cultures approach allows the connections and contradictions between individual preferences and social understandings to be explored and confronted. It investigates ways in which the various interests of motorists can be acknowledged and taken into account. This may have implications for the way people behave in cars, but it is first of all about raising awareness of the beliefs and assumptions that driving cultures construct and the dangerous consequences they may have. It requires engaging with people as rational agents in a democratic way. It also requires applying a level of reflection to a practice we take for granted and about which we are rarely challenged.

## The Value of Ideas

Driving Cultures uses a cultural change approach which we have called the "cultural learning approach." The cultural learning approach focuses on the interpersonal to deal with specific socially and culturally interactive activities, in this case driving. Working in groups, participants examine the culture and underlying beliefs, expectations and assumptions, both social and individual, implicit in driving. The cultural learning approach emphasizes participation and peer learning in an interactive framework of facilitated discussion and analysis of the social nature of activities such as driving and the contradictory meanings and expectations that inform them. The aim of the approach is to produce a space for safe reflection in order to assess and improve cultural practices.

The cultural learning process has been developed for the purpose of facilitating guided discussion and critical thinking about the practice of driving (Redshaw, 2001). It examines the implications of driving practices that are seen as problematic, but for which there is a high level of community acceptance, such as speeding. The justification given for these practices expresses community or cultural attitudes that can then be problematized. The approach combines the principles of humanities teaching and research with other learning technologies and applies them to a social problem, in this case road safety.

The importance of the cultural learning approach is that it has been identified as a conceptual framework for investigating and facilitating cultural change. The concept has been presented elsewhere with the copyright symbol to show that it is important intellectual capital. The question of intellectual property rights is controversial and cannot be addressed in this chapter. Notwithstanding the validity of those debates (see, for example, Drahos & Braithwaite, 2002; Lessig, 2002), the copyright symbol has been a useful tool in negotiations with road safety industry stakeholders who might otherwise dismiss a group discussion process as insubstantial compared with, say, the skill development involved in learning to drive. I have also applied the trade mark symbol to the Driving with a Difference™ workshop.

The workshop is a potentially marketable product, but it is important to keep in mind that it is also potentially beneficial to the community. The important point here is that it requires some effort to apply a value to intellectual capital and to make it stand out within particular contexts. An approach that looks at cultures of driving rather than individual drivers has great potential in informing education campaigns and programs. Making money from it is not the only concern, or even the most important one. Making the workshop available is the primary aim. Considering how this can be done with some financial return to the university is secondary.

Although clearly consonant with the objectives of the knowledge economy, we need to avoid reductive understandings of industry–university collaboration that assume an economic bottom line and ignore the generative role of collaboration in knowledge creation. We should not underestimate the danger of research partnerships "being framed by an instrumentalist, often commercial or merely practical horizon of expectations" (Ang, 1999, p. 8), particularly while the nature of these collaborations is maintained within traditional academic terms. Equally, we should not underestimate the dangers of insularity, of assuming that the only worthwhile knowledge is knowledge produced in the academy, and that other knowledge producers have nothing to contribute. Nor should we assume that the humanities has nothing to offer industry.

Driving Cultures was not commissioned research nor was it developed in collaboration with an industry partner. Indeed, potential opportunities for collaboration with industry and entrepreneurial activities were not immediately apparent. The project was initially funded by the New South Wales Attorney-General's Office Crime Prevention Division's Innovative Grants Scheme, which was looking for innovative ideas and the opportunity to fund their initial development. The success of the pilot led to funding from the Australian Research Council and a partnership with a motoring organization, the National Roads and Motorist Association Motoring and Services (NRMA). Our partnership with the NRMA has brought us in touch with the real and contradictory concerns of the driving public and the ways in which government and other organizations are responding to road safety issues. The partnership puts considerable resources at the disposal of both the university and the partner organization in clearly defined ways.

Collaboration is a consultative process that requires becoming familiar with the knowledge and understanding that stakeholders already possess, seeing them as possessors and producers of knowledge, and developing a research agenda that is mutually agreeable and manageable. Each party involved brings a unique knowledge base to the process. All of these knowledge bases are important. Each can make an important contribution to effecting significant social initiatives. Furthermore, because the cultural learning approach asks different questions about road safety issues to those posed by science disciplines, it can generate further research across disciplines. How, for example, might quantitative methodologies better accommodate the range of meanings that exist within the driving community? The current push towards commercialization requires investigation and examination in relation to specific projects and opportunities and how they are carried out, rather than assuming a fundamental opposition between economic and academic agendas.

## Imagining the Future

Clearly, an engagement with the social in the context of business, government, and community organizations offers the arts and humanities the prospect of responsiveness to *community* interests and concerns that will result in different kinds of benefits for communities. As indicated above, knowledge creation is becoming a more socially engaged process. The values that are becoming increasingly important include participatory decision making, community interaction, plurality, empowerment, and equity (Nowotny et al., 2002). These values, I have argued, have been limited by the traditional Enlightenment and liberal emphasis on the separation of knowledge from social and cultural contexts, standardization, and normalization—ironically, a conception of knowledge that humanities research has critiqued and sought to go beyond.

There is not necessarily an opposition between academia and commerce and other potential partners. Yet, too often, research with commercial applications is branded as "opportunistic," and arguments in favor of engagement with business and industry are dismissed as nothing more than "New Age business babble," to which the only alternative is "honorable poverty" (Adler, 2001, online). Notions of "entrepreneurialism" and "innovation" do not have to be reduced to economic buzzwords. They can be shaped in significant ways by future research if we are prepared to look critically at the way our own limited understandings contribute and how our repugnance at the commercialization of higher education and research contributes to the marginalization of the arts and humanities. "Entrepreneurial" can signify opportunities for social development, for helping people to live better lives, but to succeed in this means showing that the arts and humanities are important, relevant, and prepared to embrace new challenges.

This means making the work of the humanities known to the policy planners and producers, to demonstrate how humanities research relates to national innovation systems and knowledge economy priority research areas. It is likely that, for the time being, science will attract more funding and infrastructure. However, new frameworks of knowledge are emerging as alternatives within which partnerships can be imagined and collaboratively developed. *Imagining* the future of humanities higher education and research has to start with academe itself. How commercialization, innovation, community participation, and the uses of knowledge are re-*imagined* will determine how well or how badly the humanities fare. It is possible to shape the future contribution of the humanities to knowledge creation in favorable ways, not just for a knowledge economy, but beyond.

## Note

1. The Driving Cultures projects are conducted by Dr. Sarah Redshaw and Dr. Zoe Sofoulis at the Centre for Cultural Research, School of Cultural Histories and Futures, University of Western Sydney, Nepean, New South Wales, Australia.

## References

Adler, L. (2001). Bonfire of the humanities. *The Age*, 3 August, available online http://www.publicuni.org/?doc=theage&print=view

Ang, I. (1999). *Who needs cultural research?* Working papers. Cambridge, MA: Consortium of Humanities Centers and Institutes.

Benhabib, S. & Cornell, D. (eds.) (1987). *Feminism as critique: Essays on the politics of gender in late capitalism*. Oxford: Basil Blackwell.

Bordo, S. (1987). *Flight to objectivity: Essays on Cartesianism and culture*. Albany: State University of New York Press.

Bullen, E., Robb, S., & Kenway, J (2004) "Creative destruction": Knowledge economy policy and the future of the arts and humanities in the academy. *Journal of Education Policy* 19, (1),3-22.

Cooper, S., Hinkson, J. & Sharp, G. (eds.) (2002). *Scholars and entrepreneurs: The universities in crisis*. North Carlton, Vic: Arena Publications Association.

Coady, A. (1998). A defence of liberal knowledge. In Australian Academy of the Humanities (ed.), *Knowing ourselves and others: The humanities in Australia into the 21st century, Vol. 3, Reflective* essays (pp. 21-36). Canberra: Commonwealth of Australia.

———. (ed.) (2000). *Why universities matter*. St. Leonards: Allen and Unwin.

Connolly, W. (1991). *Identity/difference: Democratic negotiations of political paradox*. Ithaca, NY: Cornell University Press.

———. (1995). *The ethos of pluralization*. Minneapolis: University of Minnesota Press.

Drahos, P. & Braithwaite, J. (2002). *Information feudalism: Who owns the knowledge economy?* London: Earthscan.

Gaita, R. (2002). The university: Is it finished? In S. Cooper, J. Hinkson, & G. Sharp (eds.), *Scholars and entrepreneurs: The universities in crisis* (pp. 91-108). North Carlton, Vic: Arena Publications Association.

Gibbons, M. (1994). Innovation and the developing system of knowledge production. Summer Institute on Innovation, Competitiveness and Sustainability in the North American Region, Centre for Policy Research on Science and Technology, available online http://edie.cprost.sfu.ca/summer/papers/Michael.Gibbons.html

Gibbons, M., Limoges, C., Nowotny, H., Schwartzman, S., Scott, P., & Trow, M. (1994). *The new production of knowledge: The dynamics of science and research in contemporary societies.* London: Sage.

hooks, b. (1994). *Outlaw culture: Resisting representations.* New York: Routledge.

Lessig, L. (2002). *The future of ideas: The fate of the commons in a connected world.* New York: Vintage Books.

Lloyd, G. & Gatens, M. (1999). *Collective imaginings: Spinoza, past and present.* London: Routledge.

Mohanty, C.T. (2002). "Under western eyes" revisited: Feminist solidarity through anticapitalist struggles. *Signs: Journal of Women in Culture and Society, 28* (2), 499–536.

Nowotny, H., Scott, P., & Gibbons, M. (2002). *Re-thinking science: Knowledge and the public in an age of uncertainty.* Cambridge: Polity Press.

OECD (1996). *The knowledge-based economy.* Paris: OECD.

——(2002). *Dynamising national innovation systems.* Paris: OECD.

Parker, D., West, R., Stradling, S., & Manstead, A. (1995). Behavioural characteristics and involvement in different types of traffic accident. *Accident Analysis and Prevention, 27* (4), 571–581.

Parker, D., Manstead, A., & Stradling, S. (1995). Extending the theory of planned behaviour: The role of the personal norm. *British Journal of Social Psychology, 34,* 127–137.

Readings, W. (1996). *The university in ruins.* London: Harvard University Press.

Redshaw, S. (2001). Changing driving behaviour: A cultural approach. *Australian Journal of Social Issues, 36* (4), 315–331.

# ·10·

*Emily Potter*

---

# ECOLOGICAL BECOMING AND THE
# MARKETPLACE OF KNOWLEDGE

In a knowledge economy what is "useful" knowledge is that which will inspire innovation to profitable and makeshift ends, with an ultimate, but abstract, promise of future rewards. In knowledge economy policies, throughout the OECD, techno-scientific knowledge is the key driver of exchange, production, management, and consumption of services and commodities. Associated with this economy are the imperatives of commercialization, information and communication technologies (ICTs), and entrepreneurialism. Knowledge economy policies conceive of knowledge in terms of the production and consumption of use value. Within this paradigm, arts and humanities knowledge becomes both useless and wasteful. There are, however, other ways of conceiving knowledge. What happens, for example, if instead of a knowledge economy we consider a knowledge ecology? We have a system of complex relationships that by necessity accords equal value to the productive and the wasteful. Indeed in an ecology these distinctions refer only to stages of a process. The identities of the two are interdependent: both are each other in different stages of becoming. In a knowledge ecology, humanities knowledge is no more or less wasteful than techno-scientific knowledge. To consider the higher education environment in these terms enables the realization of a different view of disciplines, fields of research, and knowledge itself—not in competition or autonomously individualized, but as inter-implicated in a space of knowledge-becoming. It is this necessary and mutual coexistence of differences that thinking ecologically allows us to explore. To do so I will draw on theoretical research on ecological thinking—in particular the work of Guattari (2000), discuss the ancient agora as an example of a market located within an ecology, and, finally, consider the work of artist and academic Paul Carter as an example of an arts/humanities practice located within a market ecology.

## The Ideal Market and the University

In an episode of the BBC comedy *Yes, Minister*, civil servant Sir Humphrey Appleby explains "the four word trick" that is a certain means of inducing a Cabinet Minister to either accept or reject a policy proposal. In the first instance, these words are "quick, simple, popular, cheap," while in the second, "complicated, lengthy, expensive, controversial" should do the job (BBC 1980). Appleby's cynical reflections on the British politician spark recognition in the Australian policy climate of today, where the drive for "quick" and "simple" rather than complex responses to policy issues attests to more than the politician's primary imperative of popularity and administrative "success" in the immediate, regardless of future consequences. It is the logic of the market economy that is also invoked in the binary between complexity and efficiency, or at least the ideal market as it is rhetorically imagined in dominant post-industrial capitalist discourse.

From the language of the OECD (1996), to the Australian federal government's latest policy statement on research and development *Backing Australia's Ability* (Commonwealth of Australia, 2001) to the terminology now used in university organization and student administration, we see the same Darwinian ethic of marketplace survival. University students are "exposed to the forces of supply and demand" (Dodd & Martin, 2003, p. 6); researchers represent "human capital" (Peters, 2002, p. 137); while the "securing [of] benefits," the pursuit of "excellence" (Hall, 2003, p. 35), and the "practice of capturing, sharing and using knowledge" (OECD n.d. b) provide a solid "base" or "drive" from where economic advancement can occur. Far from knowledge disappearing from a scale of economic value, it retains a high profile as a prerequisite for profitability. In a world of depleting resources, knowledge offers an economy of "abundance" (Peters, 2002, p. 137) through consolidation and growth in a linear mode.

Knowledge economy discourses delimit not only the meaning of knowledge, but also its activity under a transcendental signifier of use value. "Use-inspired research" (OECD n.d. a) is seen as the key to economic bounty, which in turn is discursively linked to social and cultural progress. What is "useful" is that which will inspire innovation to lucrative and temporary ends, with an ultimate, but abstract, promise of future rewards. Consequently, higher education policy is infused with what universities *must* do; how they can "improve their business savvy" (Hall, 2003, p. 35), map out leading roles and paths of progress, and attain a market equilibrium between supply, demand, and exact exchange. Chika Anyanwu's description (this volume) of the global economy as a "wheel of change" wherein "a broken spoke can make an annoying clanking noise" but may not be able "to stop the wheel's motion" articulates the need for coherence and compatibility in this economic system. Once broken, a spoke in this wheel is not only useless but also anachronistic, out of place and time in an economy premised on "the right mix" of knowledge and market participation. Evoking the maxim of survival of the fittest in the competitive market, the out-of-place-ness of the clanking spoke highlights the order assumed in a well-oiled economy. Here, an economic *and* knowledge-producing community fits together in an ideal productive capacity. Wasted or useless elements therefore do not belong; they disturb the balance of the "capitalist consensus" (Pindar & Sutton, 2000, p. 13), where all exchanges are economically quantifiable.

This brings us to the problem of those knowledges that cannot be as easily conscripted to a use-value paradigm as those with material, measurable, and utility-based qualities. The techno-sciences and other selected applied and vocational disciplines are the "priority areas" of knowledge economy policy. In the background of this policy platform, humanities and creative arts knowledges are often reduced to the status of the unworkable and redundant. However, what requires interrogation is the rhetorical logic of the knowledge economy itself and its prescriptive blindness to an *ecology* in process within which knowledges, as constituents, refuse the order and calculations that an ideal economy imposes.

### Grounded Economies

An ecology, as opposed to an economy, has room and "use" for ill-fitting or disturbing elements. For Guattari in *The Three Ecologies* (2000), the existence of life on earth is dependent on seeing ecologically rather than economically. But to engage with our surroundings through "eco-logic," as he terms it, is to carefully envision an expansive, non-linear field in which complexity, ambiguity, and inconclusivity are generative forces (rather than disruptive of profitable production). An ecology is a "place" where nothing is wholly and finally ordered. In this understanding of an ecology, what becomes waste is never outside the space of our living, but moves and is part of it in incalculable ways.

Guattari's eco-logic foregrounds relation, and it is the implicitly relational characteristics of a processual ecology that so clearly highlight the abstracted and atomized character of an economy conveyed in knowledge economy rhetoric. A belief in the objectivity of the market, ideally free from regulation and state intervention, condones the abrogation of responsibility for how the market affects social and cultural life and why it has such effects. This ungrounds the commodity from the environment of its production and circulation, and disconnects effect from event. Eco-logic challenges an imagined condition of knowledge as whole and discrete with its emphasis on relation as a *condition* of singularity, which is pre-individual and pre-personal (Pindar & Sutton, 2000, p. 11). The processural nature of an ecology translates to the processes of subjectification that constitute a subject in the world as always coming into being—never natural, certain, or finished. The subject becomes in contact and "if need be, in open conflict" with the "multiple components" of its changing environment (Guattari, 2000, p. 36). Each occurrence in a processural ecology is thus "the potential bearer of new constellations of universes of reference" (Pindar & Sutton, 2000, p. 11). The generative force of ecological relations is negated in market economy rhetoric that not only individualizes, but also reduces difference to sameness in the one measure of value. This is a further paradox of an economic model that validates competition while denying singularities. As equivalences are demanded across disciplines by higher education policy, difference has become a simplistic divide between success and failure rather than an indication of aliveness and relationality.

It is important to emphasize that difference does *not* equate with atomization—where two discrete elements can be metonymically contrasted and compared—and, when considered in this light, the notion of the discipline itself is unfixed from a discourse of boundaries and limits. For instance, it is not the techno-sciences that threaten the humanities and creative arts, but the scientific paradigm through which the latter are being assessed. While the Kantian privileging of reason still influences the organizing principles of the modern university, with disciplines, departments, and faculties structured as units, the knowledges that move within the university environment constantly transgress these categories, highlighting, to again reference Guattari, "the erroneousness of dividing the Real into a number of discrete domains" (Guattari, 2000, p. 41).

Singularity relies upon, rather than precludes, connections. Indeed, as Deborah Rose (2001) points out, critical shifts in the humanities in regard to concepts of subjectivity are not isolated from or in opposition to the scientists and mathematicians who are "now rethinking all the basic principles of matter, mind, life and cosmos" (Rose, 2001, p. 32). Unlike the scientific paradigms that are inflexibly employed in higher education policy documents, many scientists work with the idea that matter is knotted and inter-related; that "[n]o longer are we atomistic singularities; we are regions, we are in connection, we are in motion, we are both cause and effect" (Rose, 2001, p. 39). Guattari agrees with this when he writes that "[p]aradoxically, it is perhaps in the 'hard' sciences that we encounter the most spectacular reconsiderations of processes of subjectification" (2000, p. 40). This could explain why, as much as the humanities and creative arts are suffering in the current policy climate in Australian universities, areas of "pure research" in the sciences and social sciences, including mathematics, chemistry, and physics, are also under pressure (Macintyre, 2002, p. 87). This is the case even though laboratory-based disciplines receive 2.35 times the funding of non-laboratory disciplines in the current Australian university regime.

The generative and transformative aspects of knowledge are absent from knowledge economy equations. Like matter, disciplines are never discrete. Knowledges are messy; they transcend sharp edges and become "processural lines of flight" (Guattari, 2000, p. 44). As an ecology involves both singularity and relations, such a way of seeing knowledge within the university environment enables modes of thought and practice to retain their importance as distinct, but not separate from, others, without hierarchy or metonymic linkage, and, importantly, as constantly in process. Such "lines" cross over and brush against each other, generating new life—or, as Guattari puts it ecologically, reinvented "modalities of 'group being'" (2000, p. 34). Knowledge, in this understanding, is always in touch with (becoming) worlds of life, and eluding totality always exists in the midst of happening.

It is the messiness of ecological knowledge that has seen the humanities and creative arts, among other disciplines, excluded from the knowledge economy paradigm, as they most overtly reveal, even celebrate, partiality and the inconclusive in processes of thought. Mess is useless in a streamlined paradigm of production and profit and, as Hawkins and Muecke (2003, p. x) contend, is reduced to the status of waste for its ambiguity, its refusal to be contained in ordered compartments. Mess, as a tangle of interrelations and points of departure and gathering, cannot be *named* in a taxonomic sense. This view prompted Hodge (1995) to use the term "monstrous knowledge" in reference to the "new humanities." Yet it is through this quality of uncertainty of value and the generation of disturbances and disequilibrium in the techno-scientific frame of rhetoric that a knowledge ecology demonstrates its aliveness.

Before I consider an alternative imagining of the market as it operates in an ecology, a final point must be made in regard to Guattari's distinction between the logic of the capitalist economy and eco-logic. In the place of scientific paradigms as ways of conceptualizing the ecological element in the world, Guattari institutes the aesthetic that he sees as accordant with the imperative to reinvent and resingularize knowledge and being-ness. Aesthetics, as poetics, are ecological to the extent that they are modes of engagement or relation, and thus bring the self into different configurations of subjectivity, which then generate meanings and reconfigure environments. Economic value cannot be supplanted by aesthetic value, and this is not Guattari's intention. What aesthetics offer is the ability to perceive and articulate the indeterminacy of value, introduced "by the gap or moment when value is yet to be decided" (Hawkins & Muecke, 2003, p. x). This is a "space" where possibilities and different configurations of being are illuminated. Thus, Hawkins and Muecke continue, "value is neither the province of the economy nor of culture, but is constantly moving between the two in multiple sites and registers" (2003, p. xi). It is this movement between differences and the generative spaces between them that we see when we consider the market in terms of an ecology, and it is in the ancient agora that this idea becomes possible.

### A Different Kind of Marketplace

Paul Carter's concept of the agora elaborates a space in which culture and economy are not divorced, but restlessly move together in a processural ecology. The ancient Roman agora was a marketplace. The variant meanings of the word, however, indicate additional ways of conceptualizing its function. "Agora" means "open space," without firm or fixed boundaries. It also refers to "an assembly of the people," and a place of "speech, oration or proclamation" (Carter, 2002, p. 31). In effect, all manner of meetings and exchanges took place in the agora: transactions occurred and commodities were bought and sold. Yet the openness of the agora (agoraphobia is a fear of open spaces, after all) profoundly alters the market's topography—its dimensions, its relations, and its poetic meaning. The agora, Carter argues, resisted "geometrical idealization" (2002, p. 185). Neither a square nor a street with defined lines and exact corners, it was a "passage-place" (2002, p. 185), a space in which subjects, objects, ideas, words, pasts, and presences converged in unordered and momentary ways. As the agora takes form and reforms through daily processes it performs the condition of knowledge as becoming, and thus as something always active in the immediate.

Poetically the agora demonstrates the insecurity of the subject and the commodities they proffer in the process of drift and becomings. It also emphasizes the distance *between* singularities, as they also continually shift into proximity and touch. The agora will not be ordered in accordance with knowledge economy logic. It exists as "a mobile arrangement of parts whose pattern can never be fully represented" (Carter, 2002, p. 138), and this poetic indeterminacy refers to the necessary incompleteness of meanings and knowledges in an ecology.

Value in the agora thus takes on the contingency described by Hawkins and Muecke. There is nothing intrinsically value-full generated here, even while structures of power as they are imagined and lived release disproportionate and often damaging effects. The agora is consequently not an ideal space and, as Carter suggests, must be historicized as such. "In its centripetal mode," he argues, "it displaces, enslaves and amalgamates," while in its "centrifugal aspect it colonizes, spreading its ideas, preoccupations and anxieties beyond the horizon" (2002, p. 15). However, in the mutability of such expansion and contraction, the imperial movements outwards and the acts of repression or exclusion inflicted from within are, like an economy, still ecologically situated. They are indeterminate and ambiguous in their realization in the world, unable to capture the desired commodity in total. Thus, as the traffic of the agora "both transforms and uplifts" ecological elements, "it also threatens to sweep away and destroy" (2002, p. 150). "[I]nflation and deflation dangerously stalk each other," Carter observes. "In the marketplace, one can talk products up, but there is always the danger that the bottom will drop out of the market" (2002, p. 150).

To imagine academic work in an agora-like market, where knowledge, even configured as a commodity, has no certain destination or concrete stance, is to challenge the rhetoric of knowledge economy policy while acknowledging the uncertainty of market operations in a complex environment. It is to imagine an economy ecologically. I turn now to some work by Paul Carter as an example of an arts/humanities practice located within this disruptive and generative space of a market ecology.

### Knowledge in the World

Paul Carter's work, both academic and artistic, has largely concerned itself with spatial, or topographical history. His work, including *The Road to Botany Bay* (1987), *The Lie of the Land* (1996) and *Repressed Spaces: The Poetics of Agoraphobia* (2002) is about relationships between space, time, colonization, and historical events. It concerns itself with a poetics of movement (Lindsey, 1996). We can see in Carter's recent public art works a poetics of the agora. These works speak of the agora in terms of relationships, ideas, public space, and becomings. They do not in themselves represent a model for all arts and humanities, nor do they model an entire ecology between ideas and the market. Rather, they are ways of beginning to think through the notion of a knowledge ecology. The starting point here is the ground, the space we inhabit, the culture and the language of that inhabitation and the interactions, or becomings possible, at that site. In this sense we are dealing with a knowledge ecology.

Here there is an interaction between identities, cultures, and place. It is in this notion of a located, relational knowledge, both abstract and grounded, that we can begin to think differently about the "place" of knowledge, and the place of the "market."

In his *Tracks* project (2003) on North Terrace, Adelaide, and the ground-work, *Nearamnew*, at Federation Square, Melbourne,[1] Carter brings varied cultural, disciplinary, and environmental knowledges into relation in a situated space open to public passage and motion. Both art works trace the human and environmental history of the sites in which they are installed, and acknowledge these spaces as topographies that are tracked with convergent and discordant "testimonies, experiences and aspirations" (Carter, *Tracks*, n.d.).

*Tracks* takes the form of eight vertical LED screens, upon which words and icons move in constant flow; and a "variable grid" ground design. Carter's own narrative constructions relating to the site are mixed with the texts of others on the screens; the images are informed by the diverse traces of the local environment, including fossilized plants, shells, and animals, and the details of indigenous rock art. The grid elaborates the colonial vision, informed by a similar logic to that of the knowledge economy, of an environment "uniform and universal, calculated to produce the most rapid and most equitably distributed investment and occupation" (Carter, *Tracks*, n.d.). for a new empire outpost.

**FIGURE 4:** Paul Carter, Tracks, design concept for an artwork at North Terrace, 2002, *Image: Buroplus.*

**FIGURE 5:** Paul Carter (in collaboration with Lab architecture studio) Nearamnew, Federation Square, detail of 'Deakin's Vision' regional ground figure, 2002, *Photo: Paul Carter.*

Yet, as Carter's grid also suggests, the regularity desired by Adelaide's first city planners was thwarted by the qualities of the local stone that "proved too crumbly to cut and dress into standard sizes and shapes . . . no two blocks were alike" (Carter, *Tracks*, n.d.).

Similarly, *Nearamnew*'s nine separate ground texts, spread around Federation Square, enact the meeting and overlapping of viewpoints and lives over time. Here, "we have the 'vision' of the maker, the colonist, the child, Alfred Deakin,[2] the migrant, the builder, the artist, the ferryman and the visitor" (Backhouse, 2001, p. 17). But in both these design works the tracks placed here do not finalize the meanings and understandings of the sites. What is vital to Carter's work is the engagement of others who pass through the space, and the living-ness of the environment in which the works are placed. As Megan Backhouse comments on *Nearamnew*, the "stone inscriptions . . . are already being touched, trodden on and rained over, which is precisely what . . . Carter had in mind" (2001, p. 17). It is the drift of people and elements around and over *Tracks* and *Nearamnew* that continues to generate meanings, in the *act* of passing through, perhaps even of ignoring their presence, or loitering nearby. These are works that "simultaneously analyse and produce subjectivity" (Guattari, 2000, p. 68) and, via their situation *in* public space, Carter's designs and the world of their surroundings enact the ecological movement of knowledges that, as some would have it, are cordoned off from relevance in university "ivory towers."

Moreover, *Tracks* and *Nearamnew* materialize the "hidden work" (see Susan Luckman, this volume) that is discounted in knowledge economy rhetoric. In so doing they affirm through performance—the encounter between foot and ground, the meeting of officially disparate lines—the processes and presence of knowledge-becoming. This performance is outside the rhetoric of economic structures, and without the need of classifications and markers. There are no signs in either design directing passers-by to meaning. As part of an ecology, *Tracks* and *Nearamnew* continue to shift and become. They are grounded works, poetically as well as literally. Their meaning comes from the environment in which they participate, but extends, in this immediacy, into other knowledges, other singularities. This is the kind of arts/humanities work that comes from thinking not in terms of a knowledge economy but rather a knowledge ecology.

## Conclusion

Knowledge and its generation are neither simplistic nor predictable, and to treat them as such is to ignore the ecological conditions *and* possibilities of our living. Relation rather than separation is the momentum of becoming. What the economy itself demonstrates, however, is that uncertainty and disequilibrium are characteristic forces of an ecology, despite the rhetoric of uniformity, which cannot arrest effects, but can only conceptually refuse them. In the market of the agora, as relations are dynamically unordered, what becomes in such a place of gathering will not be wholly quantified or made commensurable in value.

The process of knowledge-becoming does not conform to the abstracted lines of knowledge economy policy, and always spills over its ideological edges. What is "wasted" in a knowledge economy paradigm is never outside an ecology in process, but moves and relates with singular momentum—untimely, unpredictable, and transformative. To think aesthetically, as Guattari exhorts us to, foregrounds relations as the premise of all singularities, opening up generative spaces in which the different works of a culturally, historically, and topographically located academy can participate.

## Notes

1. North Terrace and Federation Square are both public cultural precincts within Australian capital cities.
2. The second Prime Minister of Australia, and a leading advocate of Federation.

## References

Backhouse, M. (2001). Inscriptions in stone take on new meaning. *The Age*, 4 August, p. 17.

BBC (1980). *Yes, Minister*. Episode 6, The right to know. Directed by S. Lotterby.

Carter, P. (1987). *The road to Botany Bay: An essay in spatial history*. London: Faber and Faber.

———. (1996). *The lie of the land*. London: Faber and Faber.

———. (2002). *Repressed spaces: The poetics of agoraphobia*. London: Reaktion.

———. (n.d.). *Tracks*. Comfort Levels Website, http://www.comfortlevels.com/current/tracks/index/htm

———. (n.d.). *Nearamnew*, available online http://www.comfortlevels.com/current/nearamnew/index.htm (accessed 18 August 2003)

Commonwealth of Australia (2001). *Backing Australia's ability: An innovation action plan for the future*. Canberra: Commonwealth of Australia.

Dodd, T. & Martin, C. (2003). Who wins, who loses in the higher education shake-out. *The Australian*, 2 April, pp. 5–6.

Guattari, F. (2000). *The three ecologies*, trans. I. Pindar & P. Sutton. London and New Brunswick, NJ: Athlone Press.

Hall, K. (2003). Research on the market. *The Australian*, 2 April, p. 35.

Hawkins, G. & Muecke, S. (2003). Cultural economies of waste. In G. Hawkins and S. Muecke (eds.), *Culture and waste: The creation and destruction of value* (pp. ix–xvii). Oxford: Rowman and Littlefield.

Hodge, B. (1995). Monstrous knowledges: Doing PhDs in the new humanities. *Australian Universities Review*, 2, 25–39.

Lindsey, K. (1996). Creative cartographies: Notes on an interview with Paul Carter. *Australian Humanities Review*, April, available online http://www.lib.latrobe.edu.au/AHR/archive/Issue-April-1996/Lindsey.html

Macintyre, S. (2002) "Funny you should ask for that": Higher education as a market. *Arena*, 17–18. 79–89.

OECD (Organization for Economic Cooperation and Development) (1996). *The knowledge-based economy in 1996: Science, technology and industry outlook*. Paris: OECD.

———. (n.d. a). Educational research and development in England: Examiner's report. OECD Website, http://www.oecd.org.dataoecd/17/56/1837550.pdf (accessed 22 August 2003).

———. (n.d. b). OECD Knowledge Management Project: Knowledge management in France. OECD Website, http://www.oecd.org/dataoecd.23/ 32/2756452/pdf (accessed 22 August 2003).

Peters, M. (2002). The university in the knowledge economy. *Arena*, *17–18*, 137–151.

Pindar, I. & Sutton, P. (2000). Translators' introduction. In F. Guattari, *The three ecologies* (pp. 1–20). London and New Brunswick, NJ: Athlone Press.

Rose, D.B. (2001). Connecting with ecological futures. In Department of Education, Training and Youth Affairs (ed.), *National Humanities and Social Sciences Summit, 2001, Position papers* (pp. 31–40). Canberra: Commonwealth of Australia.

## ·11·

*Stuart Cunningham*

# THE HUMANITIES, CREATIVE ARTS, AND INTERNATIONAL INNOVATION AGENDAS

Modern debates about the place of the humanities, the values they espouse, and the insights they instill—their use, in short—go back to Matthew Arnold (1869), Thomas Carlyle (1833–34), and Cardinal Newman's (1852) and Leavis' (1945) ideas of the university. More recently, postmodern criticism (Belsey, 1980; Eagleton, 1983) called into question understandings about the relationship between the humanities and humanism (Fuery & Mansfield, 1997). The emergence of the so-called new humanities (Ruthven, 1992), with their stress on growth, dynamism, interdisciplinarity, and post-humanism, challenged the liberal arts tradition. Debate was further complicated by claims of "cultural policy studies" about the role of the humanities in higher education in the 1990s, and intensified in Australia by higher education reform. This was a debate about first principles defences of the humanities against what were presented as historically, rather than philosophically, grounded, non-humanistic accounts of the humanities (see Hunter, Meredyth, Smith, & Stokes, 1991). Stokes offered an account of the history of the university in Australia that stressed its alignment with national priorities and planning. Smith talked about the way normative interventions in schooling were crucial to embedding the influence of the humanities academy.

Later, Ian Hunter and Tony Coady and Seumas Miller exchanged Foucauldian and neo-Marxist analyses of the role of the humanities. Hunter (1992) opened with "the humanities without humanism," to which Coady and Miller (1993) replied "the humanities without humans." This time, the debate is different.

This time, the broad context is the relation of the humanities and creative arts to the innovation agenda and the knowledge economy, and responses to global trends in local contexts. It is about the humanities *and* the creative arts, a crucial but little interrogated connection that is assuming center stage for reasons that are the burden of this paper, but also because of the growth and integration of creative arts courses and staff into the university system over the last decade. The debate, therefore, is not about the humanities and creative arts as the *ding an sich*—the imponderable thing in itself. The current debate is empirical, it is evidence-based, and it is about a wider set of issues concerning the new knowledge economy. It is a debate that humanists and creatives are *joining*, not initiating, and one to which this chapter seeks to contribute. In so doing, it seeks to answer the following questions: What is wrong with the standard innovation and research and development (R&D) agendas in a knowledge-based economy? Why should innovation and R&D agendas include the humanities and creative arts disciplines? How are innovation and R&D policies evolving internationally and how do they show a way ahead?

### *A Short Genealogy of the Knowledge-Based Economy, Innovation, and R&D Agendas*

The new macro-focus on the knowledge-based economy and innovation policies has been around in some form or other for a long time, certainly since the information society discussions of the 1960s and 1970s. Theorists of post-industrial society (Bell, 1976) and economists of knowledge (Machlup, 1962) and information (Porat, 1977) identified information management and knowledge generation—previously notional subdivisions of the service or tertiary industry sector—as separate economic sectors, the quaternary and quinary respectively. More recently, the focus on knowledge and innovation has been influenced by New Growth theory in economics, which points to the limitations for wealth creation of only micro-economic efficiency gains and liberalization strategies (Arthur, 1997; Romer 1994, 1995).

As a result, many governments are now attempting to advance knowledge-based economy models. This means a number of things. It implies a renewed interventionary role for the state after decades of neo-liberal small government; prioritization of innovation and R&D-driven industries; intensive re-skilling and education of the population; and a focus on universalizing the benefits of connectivity through mass ICT literacy upgrades. Every OECD economy, large or small—even emerging economies, for instance Malaysia—can try to play this game. This is because a knowledge-based economy is not based on old-style comparative factor advantages, but on competitive advantage, that is, what can be constructed out of integrated labor force, education, technology, and investment strategies. Japan, Singapore, and Finland are examples of competitive knowledge-based economies.

However, the humanities, creative arts, and social sciences as disciplinary tributaries of the knowledge economy—and the activities they typically support through education, training, and research—do not as a rule figure in national R&D and innovation strategies. The R&D effort in the United States, for instance, continues to be dominated by science-engineering-technology (SET) and particularly defense SET. In Europe, innovation and R&D policy, for the most part, remains focused on big science and technology. The exception is probably digital content creation, which is beginning to slip in as part of "technology," both at the European Union and member state level (see COR-DIS, n.d.). However, this is not currently happening through processes of explicit policy reconsideration and there are very few high-level policy documents, either on R&D or on innovation more broadly, that explicitly mention R&D for the creative industries or humanities. While there is the usual range of industry development support for creative industries (soft loans, grants, development of networks), recognition of the more particular R&D claims of humanities and creative skills and services more broadly as intermediate input into a wider range of activities, while supported in rhetoric, is not yet showing up in policy.

When the humanities and creative arts do appear in policy, it is often as a last minute concession to dogged lobbying, and they are usually damned with faint praise or condescended to with benign indifference. This has been evident in recent Australian policy making. The Chief Scientist's report *The Chance to Change* (Batterham, 2000) refers to the importance of creativity but the applications of creativity are all in science-engineering-technology. This report played a key role in the policy trajectory leading to the current federal government's innovation strategy, *Backing Australia's Ability* (Commonwealth of Australia, 2001) which, in the words of past Academy of the Humanities President Malcolm Gillies, is an "old-fashioned research=science document." Thus far, the process of developing a set of national research priorities has been similarly biased towards science and technology, although originally conceived with the view to creating priorities that were more inclusive than the very narrow set of four new science priorities required by the government in the Australian Research Council's programs in early 2001 (nanotechnology, photonics, genomics/phenomics, and complex systems). The release of

*Developing National Research Priorities: An Issues Paper* (DEST, 2002) in May 2002 offered a sliver of a promise of integration between humanities and social sciences and science and technology. It stated the intention that there would be a second round of priority setting addressed to the humanities and social sciences. But the reason given for prioritizing science and technology in the first round was simply that 75 per cent of the country's outlays in R&D go to science and technology. As of the time of publication, the second round of priority setting had not been scheduled, although a somewhat more inclusive set of priorities was announced in December 2002. I discuss these developments later in the chapter, as they take their place within the broader evolution of R&D policies internationally.

### *Why Should the Humanities and Creative Arts Disciplines Be Included in Innovation/R&D Agendas?*

"Our lives would be unimaginable without science" (Batterham, 2000, p. 9). It is tempting to counter such slogans and Stephen Soderbergh's statement on accepting his Oscar for directing *Traffic* in 2002 springs to mind: "Without art, life on this planet would be unendurable." However, we need to go beyond sloganeering and develop more nuanced and less polarized responses to the knowledge economy, responses based on a more complex picture of the sources of innovation and wealth creation. Arguably one of the most succinct of this type of response is found in the review of the learned academies commissioned by the Australian Department of Education, Science and Training:

> These disciplines [humanities and social sciences] provide the organisational, management, legal, accounting and marketing knowledge bases that are critical to successful innovation. They are the source of many of our insights into the human condition broadly, and to our understanding and managing the consequences of moving to a knowledge-based economy. (Blainey & Maloney, 2001, online)

In this chapter, however, I want to stress a more specific but still quite inclusive account that focuses not on the way humanities, creative arts, and social sciences analyze and manage the knowledge-based economy, but on their central role *in* it.

This is not to say that the creative industries and arts or humanities are coterminous. Indeed, their conflation has meant that policy recommendations for advancing the creative industries tend to be residual at best, the afterthought recompense for university humanities and social sciences when, instead, these industries should be foregrounded in policy. This, after all, is the sector that will deliver the content essential for next generation information and communication technology (ICT) sector growth, one of the five key knowledge-based economy hotspots.[1] Ironically, it is by distinguishing the creative industries from the creative arts and humanities that we can clarify the basis of the contribution of humanities and creative arts to innovation and R&D agendas. Creative production and cultural consumption are an integral part of the new economy, as are the disciplines that educate, train, and research these activities.

Creative production is not relegated to a residual position or marginal status in the new economy. Sociologists Scott Lash and John Urry (1994) and business analyst John Howkins (2001) claim that creative production has become the model for new economy business practices such as outsourcing, the temporary company, the "producer" model of project management, and just-in-time teams. Rifkin (2000, pp. 163–164) predicts that cultural production will ascend to the first tier of economic life, with information and services moving to the second tier, manufacturing to the third tier, and agriculture to the fourth tier. Worldwide, the creative industries sector has been among the fastest growing sectors of the global economy. Analysts and analyses, including the OECD (1998), the United Kingdom government's Creative Industries Task Force (CITF, 2001), Rifkin (2000), and Howkins (2001), point to the crucial role they play in the new economy, with growth rates better than twice those of advanced economies as a whole. Entertainment has displaced defense in the U.S. as the driver of new technology take-up, and has overtaken defense and aerospace as the biggest sector of the U.S. economy (Rifkin, 2000, p. 161).

Yet most R&D priorities continue to reflect a science and technology led agenda at the expense of new economy imperatives for R&D in the content industries, broadly defined. The broad content industries (or "knowledge consumption services") sector derives from the applied social and creative disciplines (business, education, leisure and entertainment, media, and communications) and represents 25 per cent of the U.S. economy, whilst the new science sector (agricultural biotech, fiber, construction materials, energy, and pharmaceuticals), for example, accounts for only 15 per cent of the economy (Rifkin, 2000, p. 52). In fact, all advanced economies are consumption-driven—for example, 62 per cent of gross domestic product (GDP) in the United States and 60 per cent in Australia (see Hearn, Mandeville, & Anthony, 1998)—and the social technologies that manage consumption all derive from the social and creative disciplines. In Australia, these industries or enterprises are currently valued at $25 billion per annum—as much as the residential construction industry—and growing rapidly. In high-growth areas, like digital content and applications, they are growing at twice the rate of the overall economy. Many

Australians are involved in the creative industries, ranging from hobbyists to full-time employees and small businesspeople: 2.5 million say they work in these areas, and of those about 900,000 are paid for it.

We can no longer afford to understand the social and creative disciplines as commercially irrelevant, merely "civilizing" activities. Instead, they must be recognized as one of the vanguards of the new economy. Research and development strategies must work to catch the emerging wave of innovation needed to meet demand for content creation in entertainment, education, and health information, and to build and exploit universal networked broadband architectures in strategic partnerships with industry.

The crucial point that establishes the indivisibility of the humanities and creative arts is that the knowledge economy requires both *research* and *development*, and that the contexts, meanings, and effects of *cultural consumption*, in Rifkin's terms, could be as important for these purposes as *creative production*. Major international content growth areas, such as online education, interactive television, multi-platform entertainment, computer games, web design for business-to-consumer applications, or virtual tourism and heritage, need *research* that seeks to understand how complex systems involving entertainment, information, education, technological literacy, integrated marketing, lifestyle and aspirational psychographics, and cultural capital interrelate. They also need *development* through trialing and prototyping supported by test beds and infrastructure provision in R&D-style laboratories. They need these in the context of ever-shortening innovation cycles and greater competition in rapidly expanding global markets.

### Evolving Innovation and R&D Policies

Innovation and R&D policies are evolving. There is a growing chorus worldwide that echoes—and provides the evidence base for—the arguments being made here. At the broadest level, there is now discussion of "third generation" innovation policy (Louis Lengrand & Associés et al., 2002, which the following few paragraphs follow). I would read these policy probes as differentiating amongst *innovation value chains, innovation systems,* and *innovation ecologies.*

The first generation of innovation policy—and this remains the dominant paradigm in most political/paymaster circles, if not cutting-edge scientific ones—is based on the idea of a linear process for the development of innovations. This process begins with basic knowledge breakthroughs courtesy of laboratory science and public funding of pure/basic research and moves through successive stages—seeding, pre-commercial testing, prototyping—until the new knowledge is built into commercial applications that diffuse via widespread consumer and business adoption. The prototypical industry sectors that are regarded as exhibiting these characteristics are the biotechnology and ICT sectors.

Second generation policy recognizes the complex, iterative, and non-linear nature of innovation, with many feedback loops between the different stages of the process outlined in the first generation model, and seeks to bolster the process by emphasizing the importance of the systems and infrastructures that support innovation (see, for example, OECD, 1996). These systems have focused typically on research structures and programs, education, taxation, intellectual property rights, and competition policy, and they have typically been national in their focus, emanating as they do from national governments. Innovation policies worldwide are overwhelmingly a mix of first and second generation.

Third generation innovation thinking is based on ecological more than systems paradigms. The systems have to be brought into interaction with each other, and a deeper, longer-term as well as wider view needs to be taken. Innovation depends on organizational, social, economic, marketing, and other knowledge. There is an increasing recognition that tying, say, the education system to innovation does not necessarily address the root causes of a lack of innovativeness in that system as a whole. Each of the systems themselves need to be subject to innovation strategies, and brought into a closer relation to each other. Innovation needs to be more grassroots, at regional and sectoral levels as much as national.

To flesh this out a little, take an example from the SET heartland. To turn children on to science and mathematics—a goal of innovation policy in the United Kingdom, Australia, and elsewhere—rich, innovative, games-based products that are, yes, *entertaining*, will be needed. C.P. Snow's "two cultures" (1964)—the gulf between science and humanities/arts—has to be bridged if the sentiments and strategies of the policy are to be realized. Another example might be how to address the structural weaknesses in skill base and business infrastructure, a preoccupation of, for example, the European Commission. These weaknesses point to the need to integrate entrepreneurialism into curricula and to foster collaborative networks and an export orientation. These values cannot be administered; they must be fostered and they relate to factors of deep culture that are not amenable to quick fix government programs. An export orientation might to a great degree depend on language and intercultural awareness. Entrepreneurialism may be best fostered outside formal schooling, not inside it.

Innovation frameworks set the broad parameters within which R&D strategies are developed. Let us now turn to evidence that such strategies are also evolving and beginning to contemplate the role of creative content.

Canada, New Zealand, Australia, and Taiwan are seeing evidence of creative industries being at least contemplated as an R&D sector and the principles for R&D intervention being compared with and not mapped onto cultural and industry intervention principles (see Cunningham, 2002, 2004). In Canada, there is some interesting work on stimulating Canada's broadband content industry through R&D strategies (Delvinia, 2001). In New Zealand, the Foundation for Research, Science and Technology is promulgating explicit R&D policy for the creative industries, identified as a national "Growth and Innovation Framework" priority along with biotechnology and ICT.

In Australia, the National Research Priorities (NRP) process requires publicly funded research bodies,[2] and therefore all the major research facilities and infrastructure at a national level, to take account of these priorities and report on their acquittal of them. One of them is "frontier technologies for building and transforming Australian industries." In this priority area there are key statements such as "research is needed to exploit the huge potential of the digital media industry" (DEST, 2003, online), and a number of examples of content applications such as e-commerce, multimedia, content generation, and imaging are mentioned for priority research and development. This emerging framework arguably provides fertile ground for the first cooperative research center in creative digital content and applications (the Australasian Centre for Interaction Design, with Queensland University of Technology Creative Industries as the lead site) awarded in 2002. Further changes to the NRP may see greater articulation of priorities amenable to humanities and creative arts.

In the context of a National Development Plan, Taiwan is proposing to adopt a more "humanistic and sustainable" approach to the development of "culturally creative industries," the goals of which are to nurture creative skills and promote the combination of culture with entrepreneurship to develop cultural industries. The plan explains that "This necessitates setting up an organization to promote culturally creative industries, cultivating creative manpower for art and design, molding an environment conducive to the development of creative industries and developing creative design and culture-based industries" (Taiwan, 2002, online). The plan includes investing in the more high-tech end of the creative industry spectrum, major new R&D investment, establishing specialized schools in such key areas as ICT design and digital content, and encouraging cooperation among industry, academia, and research institutions.

While the U.S. R&D effort continues to be dominated by science-engineering-technology and particularly defense SET, *Beyond Productivity* is a good example of a probe from the National Academy searching for purchase for an investment strategy for the digital arts and design based on innovation (Mitchell, Inouye, & Blumenthal, 2003). As we have seen, digital content creation is also beginning to appear as part of technology R&D in Europe. The European Commission's influence over R&D in member states is driven to a large extent by direct funding of its research priorities under the various Framework programs. If the commission is showing an interest in funding digital content research (which it is), it does not mean member states will adopt that policy, but that research will get funded in those countries and will lead to pressure on national research bodies to support similar activities.

The current research program is the Sixth Framework Program and it is organized into thematic areas. Most are still science and technology-focused, but there are two areas—"information society technologies" and "citizens and governance in a knowledge-based society"—that will directly support arts and humanities research. "Information society technologies" includes two categories of direct relevance: "cross-media content for leisure and entertainment," and "technology-enhanced learning and access to cultural heritage."

Research and development is a live issue in the humanities and creative arts research community in the United Kingdom. On one hand, the Arts and Humanities Research Board is to be made into a full Research Council, with the same status as the others that deal with science and technology (and in the case of the Economic and Social Research Council with social sciences). On the other hand, the same White Paper on higher education (DfES, 2003) makes almost no other mention of either the arts or the creative industries. Nor do most of the Department for Trade and Industry policy statements on the knowledge economy.

*Concluding Challenges*

In this chapter I have rehearsed the challenges and changes facing traditional science-based innovation frameworks and R&D strategies. There is, of course, a reverse challenge—for the humanities and creative arts. We need to sharpen our understanding and use of the term R&D. Research and development is not just anything we decide it to be in an opportunistic move to add another public outlay pot to the already established ones of cultural and education subsidy. A second and related challenge is to see to what extent we can achieve the kind of scale and coordination expected of the sciences in the national interest. Is it appropriate, or are we endemically (or as a matter of principle) to be considered small-scale, fragmented, cottage-industry researchers?

Third, we do not stand outside of our objects of study. My argument about the relevance to innovation of the content and creative industries—and the disciplines that study them—reminds us that we are part of what we study (for example, the education industry). This is a conceptual and political shift that presents a major challenge if we continue to think of the humanities and creative arts as constitutively oppositional and individual, and deserving of public subsidy *because* of our oppositionality (the conscience of the nation) and exceptionalism (acquitted with individual brilliance and excellence). Before we are recognized as contributing to the global knowledge economy and our national innovation systems, we must innovate through changing ourselves.

## Notes

1. ICT is seen as one of five key knowledge-based economic growth hotspots into the future, along with biotechnology, environmental management, medical services, and education export.
2. The Australian Research Council (ARC), the Commonwealth Scientific and Industrial Research Organization (CSIRO), the National Health and Medical Research Council (NHMRC), and the defense and nuclear science R&D organizations.

## Acknowledgments

I would like to thank Kate Oakley for intelligence on the European R&D scene, and Sal Humphreys and Michael Keane for research assistance on world trends in innovation and R&D.

## References

Arnold, M. (1869). *Culture and anarchy*. Cambridge, UK: Cambridge University Press (1960 edition).

Arthur, B. (1997). Increasing returns and the new world of business. In J. Seely Brown (ed.), *Seeing differently: Insights on innovation* (pp. 3–18). Boston: Harvard Business Review Books.

Batterham, R. (2000). *The chance to change*. Canberra: Commonwealth of Australia.

Blainey, G. & Maloney, J.E. (2001). *2000 Review of the Australian learned academies*. Canberra: Commonwealth of Australia, available online http://www.dest.gov.au/highered/respubs/academies/default.htm

Bell, D. (1976). *The coming of post-industrial society: A venture in social forecasting*, 2nd ed. New York: Basic Books.

Belsey, C. (1980). *Critical practice*. London: Methuen.

Carlyle, T. (1833–34). *Sartor Resartus*. New York: Oxford University Press (1999 edition).

CITF (Creative Industries Task Force) (2001). Website, http://www.culture.gov.uk/creative/mapping.html

Coady, T. & Miller, S. (1993). The humanities without humans. *Meanjin, 52* (2) 391–399.

Commonwealth of Australia (2001). *Backing Australia's ability: An innovation action plan for the future*. Canberra: Commonwealth of Australia.

Community Research & Development Information Service (CORDIS) (n.d.). Website, http://www.cordis.lu

Cunningham, S. (2002). From cultural to creative industries: Theory, industry, and policy implications. *Media International Australia: Incorporating Culture & Policy, 102,* 54–65.

———. (2004). The creative industries after cultural policy: A genealogy and some possible preferred futures. *International Journal of Cultural Studies, 7* (1), 105–115.

Delvinia (2001). *Filling the pipe: Stimulating Canada's broadband content industry through R&D*. Report on the National Roundtables on Advanced Broadband Content, prepared for Canarie Inc. Toronto: Delvinia.

Department for Education and Skills (DfES) (2003). *The future of higher education,* Cm 5735. London: DfES, available online http://www.dfes.gov.uk/highereducation/hestrategy/pdfs/DfES-HigherEducation.pdf

Department of Education, Science and Training (DEST) (2002). *Developing national research priorities: An issues paper*. Canberra: DEST.

———. (2003). *Frontier technologies for building and transforming Australian industries*. National Research Priorities. Canberra: Commonwealth of Australian, available online http://www.dest.gov.au/priorities/transforming_industries.htm

Eagleton, T. (1983). *Literary theory: An introduction*. Oxford: Blackwell.

Fuery, P. & Mansfield, N. (1997). *Cultural studies and the new humanities: Concepts and controversies*. Melbourne: Oxford University Press.

Hearn, G., Mandeville, T., & Anthony, D. (1998). *The communication superhighway: Social and economic change in the digital age*. Sydney: Allen and Unwin.

Howkins, J. (2001). *The creative economy: How people make money from ideas*. London: Allen Lane.

Hunter, I. (1992). The humanities without humanism. *Meanjin, 51* (3), 479–490.

Hunter, I., Meredyth, D., Smith, B., & Stokes, G. (1991). *Accounting for the humanities: The language of culture and the logic of government*. Brisbane: Institute for Cultural Policy Studies.

Lash, S. & Urry, J. (1994). *Economies of signs and space*. London: Sage.

Leavis, F.R. (1945). *Education and the university: A sketch for an "English school."* London: Chatto & Windus.

Louis Lengrand & Associés, PREST, & ANRT (2002). *Innovation tomorrow: Innovation policy and the regulatory framework: Making innovation an integral part of the broader structural agenda*. Innovation paper No. 28, European Commission Directorate-General for Enterprise. Luxembourg: Official Publication Office of the European Communities.

Machlup, F. (1962). *The production and distribution of knowledge in the United States.* Princeton, NJ: Princeton University Press.

Mitchell, W., Inouye, A., & Blumenthal, M. (eds.) (2003) *Beyond productivity: Information technology, innovation and creativity.* Washington: National Academies Press.

Newman, J.H. (1852). *On the scope and nature of university education.* London: Dent (1965 edition).

Organization for Economic Cooperation and Development (OECD) (1996). *The knowledge-based economy.* Paris: OECD.

———. (1998). *Content as a new growth industry.* Paris: OECD.

Porat, M.U. (1977). The information economy: Definition and measurement. *Information Economy, 1,* 22–29.

Rifkin, J. (2000). *The age of access: How the shift from ownership to access is transforming modern life.* London: Penguin.

Romer, P. (1994). The origins of endogenous growth. *Journal of Economic Perspectives, 8* (1), 3–22.

———. (1995). Interview with Peter Robinson. *Forbes, 155* (12), 66–70.

Ruthven, K.K. (ed.) (1992). *Beyond the disciplines: The new humanities.* Canberra: Australian Academy of the Humanities.

Snow, C.P. (1964). *The two cultures: And a second look.* Cambridge: Cambridge University Press.

Taiwan (2002). The New Six-Year National Development Plan of Taiwan, available online http://www.roc-taiwan.or.kr/policy/20021021/2002102101.html

# ·12·

*Paul Jeffcutt*

---

# CONNECTIVITY AND CREATIVITY
# IN KNOWLEDGE ECONOMIES:
# EXPLORING KEY DEBATES

Over the past five years in particular, the significance of creativity for knowledge economies has been acknowledged as never before. Influential national (DCMS, 1998, 2001) and transnational (EC, 2001; NEF, 2002) reports have recognized the value (measured by employment and turnover) and dynamism (measured by growth) of creativity to contemporary economies. In this light, a "new" arena for policy action, the creative industries, has been constructed for the development of cities, regions, and nations.

My chapter examines this significant (and contested) arena of development for knowledge societies, arguing that connectivity is a crucial, but poorly understood, process that shapes these developments. The chapter will focus on the complex dynamics of connectivity, both operational and conceptual, drawing out key themes to enhance understanding of the knowledge and practice of creativity in contemporary economies. Reviewing problems and opportunities in the field, the chapter concludes by examining a developing research agenda.

*Operational Connectivity*

In terms of conventional indicators, the volume and value of activity in the creative industries is highly significant for western economies. For example, in the U.K. the creative industries are valued at 5 per cent of GDP (£112 billion turnover per annum—approximately 170 billion Euro), employ 1.3 million people, and are growing at twice the rate of the rest of the economy (DCMS, 2001).

The creative industries have been defined as follows: "those activities which have their origin in individual creativity, skill and talent and which have a potential for wealth and job creation through the generation and exploitation of intellectual property. These have been taken to include the following key sectors: advertising, architecture, the art and antiques market, crafts, design, designer fashion, film, interactive leisure software, music, the performing arts, publishing, software and television and radio" (DCMS, 1998).

The creative industries can thus be appreciated as a desirable feature of vitality in a knowledge society—not only valuable but also cool and sophisticated. However, what are the key dynamics that are shaping this contemporary manifestation of creativity in knowledge economies? To better understand these dynamics we need to look more closely at different processes of operational connectivity.

*Cross-Sectoral*

The creative industries are shaped by interconnection between the media/information industries and the cultural/arts sector. This is evident at all levels of activity, from the growth of new cultural entrepreneurs to the merger between Time/Warner and AOL to produce one of the world's largest corporations.

*Cross-Professional*

The creative industries are shaped by interconnection between diverse domains (or forms) of creative endeavor (i.e. visual art, craft, print, video, music, etc.) that are brought together through new opportunities for the use of digital media technologies. For example, over the past decade, the U.K. video game sector has developed from the cult activity of teenagers in suburban bedrooms to an international export industry equivalent in value to that of radio and television (DCMS, 2001).

*Cross-Governmental*

The creative industries as a policy field (at whatever level) bring together a complex network of stakeholders—departments of culture and departments of industry, trade, professional and educational bodies—to attempt effective "joined up" policy making and governance.

The outcomes of this multi-layered operational connectivity are complex and challenging. The creative industries span a diverse range of activities (i.e. arts, genres, crafts, specialisms, and domains of endeavor), all of which have creativity at their core ("where creativity is the enterprise"). This produces a terrain with a very mixed economy of forms—from micro-businesses, through micro-enterprises to transnational organizations—encompassing the range from sole artists to global media corporations. The creative process in these organizations is distinguished by a complex cycle of knowledge flows, from the generation of original ideas to their realization (whether as products or performances). As Leadbeater and Oakley (1999) argue, the creative process is sustained by inspiration and informed by talent, vitality, and commitment— this makes creative work volatile, dynamic, and risky, shaped by important tacit skills (or expertise) that are frequently submerged (even mystified) within domains of endeavor. Despite their contemporary influence and value, the crucial dynamics that form and transform the creative process in knowledge economies remain unruly and poorly understood.

In particular, there is a lack of strategic knowledge about the relationships and networks that enable and sustain the creative process in knowledge economies. These relationships are enabled between the diverse contributors to the creative process (whether engaged with the inspiration or the perspiration) toward the achievement of successful outcomes (whether realized in terms of performances or products). These relationships involve the bringing together of diverse expertise (both creative and non-creative) in complex value chains of symbolic goods that link the originators of novel ideas with the consumers of novel experiences (see Scott, 1999; Caves, 2000). These knowledge-intensive relationships are both situated and networked (see Jeffcutt & Pratt, 2002; Jeffcutt, 2003), sustained by diverse communities of activity, from project-based/hybrid/virtual organizations to cultural quarters and digital media hubs. Clearly, these diverse relationships and networks are organized, even if they may not always be managed (in conventional terms).

The challenge for researchers and policy makers is thus to understand these crucial dynamics better so that insightful and supportive action may be pursued. This challenge is all the more important in a contemporary context where the outputs of the creative industries are trumpeted (as sexy and significant) and a whole plethora of policy initiatives are being undertaken (across Europe and elsewhere), searching to expand these outcomes in the short-term. One concern is that the motivation for this activity is often the hope of joining a bandwagon (for fear of being left behind) with insufficient regard for the complexity of these creative dynamics and with little evaluation of cause and effect. Indeed, the very desirable outputs of the creative industries may even be happening in various locales *despite* (rather than because of) particular policy actions, which may actually be impeding or disrupting core creative processes. In any event, the numerous actions that are being undertaken are largely local and fragmented and are rarely being evaluated in ways that will enable the development of cumulative knowledge (within and across regions).

A remaining operational problem is that of adequately defining the creative industries. To concentrate attention on sectors where creativity is more visible in the knowledge economy does not imply that creativity is redundant in the remainder of industry. For example, in terms of the U.K. definition, science, technology, and manufacturing are primarily "non-creative" industries; however, this is not a depiction that fits the many highly inventive enterprises active in these fields (e.g. Intel, Dyson).

This section, which has reviewed the dynamics of operational connectivity for the creative industries, thus concludes with a rather double-edged message. Marking out the creative industries provides, on the one hand, a welcome emphasis on the significance and value of creativity for knowledge economies; but on the other hand, the currently dominant approach provides a rather arbitrary bounding of this creativity that diverts emphasis from key generic issues, such as the core dynamics of the creative process in knowledge economies.

## Conceptual Connectivity

The dynamics of connectivity in the intellectual context are similarly diverse and multi-layered, bringing together fields of knowledge with different approaches to the relationship between creativity and the economy. As has already been seen, contemporary approaches to the creative industries value creativity in some industrial settings, but overlook it in others. In order to explore the structures that produce this valuation, we need to reflect on the web of conceptual relationships between "culture" and "industry." As Williams (1958, 1983) and others have shown, appreciating the complexities of this relationship necessitates engagement with a diverse and longstanding intellectual heritage. In this light, the following summary does not seek to be exhaustive but illustrates that the relationship between "culture" and "industry" has typically been understood in terms of key separations (see also Jeffcutt et al., 2000) from which distinctive views can be outlined.

## Romantic: An Opposition to Cultural Decline

In the nineteenth century, alongside the development of a modern economy in Britain, Romantics (such as Coleridge and Arnold) envisaged a society led by an artistic elite who would be untainted by commerce. This influential movement rejected rationalism, celebrated individual inspiration, and opposed what they saw as cultural decline. These understandings establish a key separation between high (canonical) culture and mass (popular) culture.

### Critical Theory: The Industrialization of Leisure Time

Adorno and Horkheimer (Marxists who had fled from Germany to New York in the 1930s) developed the term "culture industry" in 1944. In a context of U.S. consumerism, they argued that culture had become industrialized through a controlling process of uniformity and predictability, akin to Fordist mass production. These critical understandings establish a key separation between mass deception and authenticity.

### Economic: Culture at the Leading Edge of Late Capitalism

As was recognized in the preceding section, the creative industries have recently become seen as a leading or privileged sector of contemporary capitalism. As was also observed, these understandings establish a key separation between aesthetic goods and non-aesthetic goods.

### Socio-Political: Culture as an Instrument of Community Regeneration

Over the last twenty years or so (in particular), the cultural or creative sector has also become seen as an instrument of community development and thus a focus of state investment, often around agendas of social inclusion. These understandings establish a key separation between socio-cultural costs and socio-cultural benefits.

Clearly the four distinct positions discussed here—romantic, critical, economic, socio-political—each incorporate their own value systems and judgements in constructing a meaning for the relationship between "culture" and "industry." However, they are also joined in important ways, for they all see the distinctions that shape the relationship between "culture" and "industry" as forming a relatively stable structure that is coherent and manageable (whether positively or negatively valued).

In contrast, a number of contemporary critical approaches would argue that the fundamentals of the interrelationship between "culture" and "industry" are blurred, unstable, and unmanageable. For example:

*Romantic.* Over the past century, artists from Duchamp to Warhol have sought to overturn the distinction between "high" and "popular" culture. Subsequently, postmodernists have argued that there can no longer be any absolute criteria of judgement—all is open to critique and debate (Hutcheon, 1989).

*Critical theory.* Baudrillard and others have suggested that the spheres of economics and of culture can no longer be realistically separated. In this "hyperreal" world there is no originary authenticity, only image and delusion. Culture is simply another form of transactional activity (Lash & Urry, 1994).

*Economic.* Recent work from anthropology (e.g. Fjellman, 1992; Miller, 2001) and consumer behaviour (e.g. Brown, 1995; Brown & Patterson, 2001) has argued that all goods are expressive and can be consumed for their aesthetic qualities, whether tractors or movies.

*Socio-political.* Recent work from cultural policy (e.g. Pick & Anderton, 1999; Mercer, 2002) has argued that state-led neo-patronage may be more effective at constraining rather than enabling creative space for community development.

Through these critiques we can see an emerging conceptual territory concerned with understanding the creative process in knowledge economies—interconnecting the arts, humanities, and social sciences. This territory extends to a range of recent work from the arenas of organizational analysis (Bjorkegren, 1996; Davis & Scase, 2000), media and cultural studies (Du Gay, 1997; Du Gay & Pryke, 2001; Hesmondhalgh, 2002), cultural policy (Pick & Anderton, 1999; Mercer, 2002), economic geography (Scott, 1999, 2000), critical anthropology (Fjellman, 1992; Miller, 2001), and consumer behavior (Brown, 1995; Brown & Patterson, 2001). Characterized by its interdisciplinarity, this range of work is linked by a concern for the dynamics of the cultural production–consumption interface in a developing economy of "signs and space."

## Creativity and Knowledge in Action

Thus far I have argued that the creative industries are characterized by dynamic contact zones that are inter-operational and interdisciplinary, providing a territory that is hybrid, multi-layered and rapidly changing. A key challenge for researchers is to develop an appropriate conceptual and organizational framework within which to focus and situate analyses of this territory—in other words, the development of a strategic framework of knowledge concerning the dynamics of the creative process in knowledge economies. Clearly, such knowledge is needed for assimilation, assessment, and to create and sustain a credible evidence base for strategic action. As has been seen, this strategic knowledge, where it exists, is currently fragmented and partial. A framework around which to build and further develop this strategic knowledge can be set out as follows.

*Micro.* Analysis of the process and craft of creative activity in different "industries," concentrating on what is distinctive about these activities in each domain of endeavor (i.e. situated knowledge, identity) and what could be identified as catalysts for creative invention and its successful translation into the processes that lead to innovative outputs.

*Meso.* Comparative analysis, across domains, of what enables and supports innovation processes in their (unruly) interface with creative invention; concentrating on these dynamics in relation to key intermediary factors for creative enterprises, such as expertise, media, networking, and organization, that impact across the territory.

*Macro.* Comparative analysis within and across cities, regions, and nations of the relationship between creative enterprises and socioeconomic development in knowledge societies; concentrating on the role of key environmental enablers annd inhibitors such as intellectual property rights, cultural diversity, skill sets and access, entrepreneurship capabilities, ICT capabilities, governance, institutional partnerships, labor markets, development policy, and funding.

*Meta.* Analysis of the longer-term impact of changes in aesthetics, lifestyle, commodification, consumption, and spatiality on the development of an evolving knowledge society (local, regional, national, and transnational).

This framework describes a broad territory, across which research activity is both dispersed and in the early stages of development. In this light, it is significant to note the following main trends. To date there has been much greater emphasis on macro (e.g. Landry, 2000) and meta (e.g. Castells, 2000) analysis, with a relative neglect of meso and (to a lesser extent) micro analysis. Significantly, there has been little joining up of analysis across levels to produce a more integrated framework of strategic knowledge.

This chapter has argued that issues of management, organization, and governance are fundamental to the strategic framework of knowledge outlined above. I have also argued that strategic knowledge in the creative industries must be situated in the analysis of particular organizational fields, not simply imported from other sectors or industries. A significant theme from the small body of research in this area is the importance of emerging organizational spaces, interfaces, and intermediaries (see Jeffcutt & Pratt, 2002; Pratt, 2002; Jeffcutt, 2003).

Over the course of the chapter, it has been seen that creative industries occupy an unruly organizational space between the domains of culture and industry, that they articulate the contested interfaces between the practices of management and creativity, and that they mobilize these complex operational interrelationships through intermediaries. These hybrid and emergent organizational spaces, made up of dynamic interfaces between multiple stakeholders with many layers of knowledge, are both characteristic of, and endemic in, the creative industries. Particularly significant has been the role of intermediaries—individuals, formations, and institutions that not only seek to broker connections at interfaces (whether between persons, parties, or knowledges), but which also seek to transform the space in which they are operating. In other words, these intermediaries have the potential to form learning or intelligent agencies, able to shape and transform the dynamic organizational spaces of the creative industries.

*Conclusion*

This chapter has reviewed key debates across a complex field concerned with creativity in knowledge economies. Concentrating on the dynamics of connectivity, both operational and conceptual, this discussion has necessarily considered a rich mix of problems and opportunities, both inter-operational and interdisciplinary.

Having considered how to build and further develop strategic knowledge in this field, a number of major challenges can be outlined. The main challenge for researchers is to insightfully analyze the ecosystem of creative space in particular knowledge economies—this is made up of multi-layered knowledge networks and transactions, and is articulated by the emerging dynamics of interconnection (i.e. clusters, interfaces, margins, and hybrids: Jeffcutt, 2003). The corresponding challenge for policy makers is to work insightfully with this situated knowledge (and its stakeholders) to enhance the creative space of particular knowledge economies. This involves an ecological approach (Jeffcutt, 2003) that is generic, integrated, and which focuses on key dynamics (i.e. enabling connections at interfaces through brokerage and intermediaries).

Evidently, the key socioeconomic issues of the twenty-first century do not come conveniently divided up in terms of pre-existing structures—hence to effectively address them we need to work in ways that are more interactive, distributed, and dynamic. Because of its dynamics of connectivity, the field concerned with creativity in knowledge economies is well prepared for boundary-crossing approaches to the development of such strategic knowledge. It is clearly a field of distributed expertise (between researchers, policy makers, and practitioners) built around multiple networks that do not value convention. It is also a field of multiple stakeholders where key questions need to be framed and reframed across contexts in an interactive process of analysis, response, and action.

Arenas that practice such strongly contextualized co-development between distributed expertise and stakeholders have been characterized as fields of "Mode 2" knowledge (Gibbons et al., 1994; Nowotny et al., 2001) and are thought to be more effective at dealing with the challenges of complexity in knowledge societies than the more traditional "Mode 1" knowledges. Within the field concerned with creativity in knowledge economies, there is a growing recognition of the importance of "Mode 2" methods of knowledge development. Recent work has included:

1. research and development networks that bring together practitioners and researchers to debate key contemporary issues (e.g. UK Forum on the Creative Industries, n.d.);
2. integrated research and development programs that bring together fundamental and applied perspectives in the development of strategic knowledge (e.g. Creative Enterprise, n.d.);
3. integrated policy initiatives that bring together stakeholders from government, industry, education, and professional bodies to take forward strategic action in cities (e.g. Cultural Industries Development Service, n.d., Manchester) and regions (e.g. Unlocking Creativity, n.d., Northern Ireland).

These actions aim to build an effective "in-between"—characterized by sustainable pathways and effective partnerships between research, policy, and practice. Such work is not only crucial for the development of creativity in knowledge economies, but also for the development of "Mode 2" knowledge.

*References*

Bjorkegren, D. (1996). *The culture business*. London: Routledge.

Brown, S. (1995). *Postmodern marketing*. London: Routledge.

Brown, S. & Patterson, A. (eds.) (2001). *Imagining marketing: Art, aesthetics and the avant-garde*. London: Routledge.

Castells, M. (2000). *The information age*. Oxford: Blackwell.

Caves, R. (2000). *The creative industries*. Harvard: Harvard University Press.

Creative Enterprise (n.d.) Web page, www.qub.ac.uk/creative

Cultural Industries Development Service (n.d.) Web page, www.cids.co.uk

Davis, H. & Scase, R. (2000). *Managing creativity*. Buckingham: Open University Press.

DCMS (1998). *The creative industries mapping report.* London: HMSO.

———. (2001). *The creative industries mapping report.* London: HMSO.

Du Gay, P. (1997). *Production of culture/cultures of production.* London: Sage.

Du Gay, P. & Pryke, M. (eds) (2001). *Cultural economy.* London: Sage.

European Commission (2001). *Exploitation and development of the job potential in the cultural sector in the age of digitalisation.* Munich: European Commission DG Employment and Social Affairs.

Fjellman, S.M. (1992). *Vinyl leaves.* Boulder, Colorado: Westview Press.

Gibbons, M., Limoges, C., Nowotny, H., Schwartzman, P., & Trow, M. (1994). *The new production of knowledge: The dynamics of science and research in contemporary societies.* London: Sage.

Hesmondhalgh, D. (2002). *The cultural industries.* London: Sage.

Hutcheon, L. (1989). *The politics of postmodernism.* London: Routledge.

Jeffcutt, P. (2003). *Creative enterprise: Developing and sustaining the creative industries in Northern Ireland.* Belfast: Centre for Creative Industry, Queen's University.

Jeffcutt, P., Pick, J., & Protherough, R. (2000). Culture and industry: Exploring the debate. *Studies in Cultures, Organizations and Societies, 6* (2), 129–143.

Jeffcutt, P. & Pratt, A. (2002). Managing creativity and the creative industries. *Creativity and Innovation Management, 11* (2), 225–233.

Landry, C. (2000). *The creative city.* Leicester: Earthscan.

Lash, S. & Urry, J. (1994). *Economies of signs and space.* London: Sage.

Leadbeater, C. & Oakley, K. (1999). *The independents.* London: Demos.

Mercer, C. (2002). *Towards cultural citizenship.* Hedemora: Gidlunds Forlag.

Miller, D. (ed.) (2001). *Consumption: Critical concepts in the social sciences.* London: Routledge.

NEF (2002). *Creative Europe.* Bonn: Network of European Foundations for Innovative Cooperation.

Nowotny, H., Scott, P., & Gibbons, M. (2001). *Rethinking science, knowledge and the public in an age of uncertainty.* Cambridge: Polity Press.

Pick, J. & Anderton, M. (1999). *Building Jerusalem.* Amsterdam: Harwood Academic Publishers.

Pratt, A.C. (2002). Hot jobs in cool places: The material cultures of new media product spaces—the case of San Francisco. *Information, Communication and Society, 5* (1), 27–50.

Scott, A. (1999). The cultural economy: Geography and the creative field. *Media, Culture and Society, 21* (6), 807–817.

———. (2000). *The cultural economy of cities.* London: Sage.

UK Forum on the Creative Industries (n.d.). Web page, www.mmu.ac.uk/h-ss/mipc/foci

Unlocking Creativity (n.d.). Web page, www.dcalni.gov.uk/publications

Williams, R. (1958). *Culture and society.* London: Chatto and Windus.

———. (1983). *Keywords.* London: Flamingo.

# ·13·

*Jane Kenway, Elizabeth Bullen, & Simon Robb*

## GLOBAL KNOWLEDGE POLITICS AND "EXPLOITABLE KNOWLEDGE"

The "knowledge economy" policy trajectory within key international and transnational organizations is the concern of this chapter. Its first purpose is to give an indication of the global policy context within which the arts and humanities in the academy are currently positioned. Its second purpose is to identify some of the differential implications of this policy context for the arts and humanities in so-called developed and developing countries respectively. To this end we focus on the knowledge economy policies of the Organization for Economic Cooperation and Development (OECD) and the World Bank. While having much in common, the former's policies are mainly concerned with developed national economies and the latter's with developing national economies. Obviously the future of the arts and humanities in the academy is linked to the future of the academy itself, which in turn is linked to the changing nature of the state in the global political order. After all, research and teaching in these fields are largely funded by the state in the context of national higher education policies. The chapter thus identifies the ways in which the state, tertiary education, knowledge and research are constructed within the policies of these two major supranational political power brokers and hints at some of the flow-on effects of such policies.

*Policy Perspectives: Global Governance and the Nation–State*

Education policy and the politics of university knowledge are conventionally studied from a national or nation–state standpoint. Yet, as Held and McGrew (2002) argue, supranational organizations have become so powerful in regard to policy development that such standpoints are no longer sufficient. An increasing number of education scholars are thus considering the implications of globalization for education policy (for example, Stromquist & Monkman, 2000; Currie & Newson, 1998; Henry et al., 2001). As such research indicates, the field of education policy studies is now moving beyond its "embedded statism" (Tomlinson, 1999) wherein the nation–state is naturalized as the "political power container" and as a primary "source of cultural identity" (1999, p. 104). Studies of education policy are now open to examining new spatialities and mobilities. Thus, they now attend to the educational implications of global flows of trade, investment, wealth, labor, people, ideas, and images. They take more seriously the porosity of national borders and its effects on national policy. National education/knowledge policies are now clearly caught up in the hegemonies and imperatives of various forms of global governance, and education policies travel, with some speed, between nation–states as well as between nation–states and inter- and transnational organizations. Given this, it is pertinent to begin with a brief introduction to the matter of global governance. This is complex and much contested terrain.

Nation–states "share the global arena and global power with international organisations, trans-national concerns and trans-national social and political movements" (Beck, 2001, p. 34). This results in what Rosenau (cited in Beck 2001, p. 35) calls "polycentric world politics." Such politics involve two main realms: "a community of states" and "trans-national sub politics." The first consists of nation–states and the conventions and power dynamics that have evolved around their interactions. The second realm consists of all those organizations that act upon the global stage, but are not rooted in the nation–state. According to Held and McGrew (2002), these organizations are rapidly increasing in number. While there is considerable debate about the extent to which the community of states is the dominant power structure and about what remains of state sovereignty, there is a general agreement that inter- and transnational or supranational links have become more and more dense and complex, thus "obscuring the lines of responsibility and accountability of nation–states themselves" (Held, quoted in Beck, 2001, p. 37).

Many international and transnational organizations are directly involved in the global politics of knowledge and concern themselves specifically with education policy, although each comes with somewhat different interests and purposes. Examples of such organizations include trade and commerce-based bodies such as the World Bank, the World Trade Organization (WTO), the International Monetary Fund (IMF) and OECD. They tend to think of education largely in economic terms. In contrast, such organizations as UNESCO, UNICEF, the European Commission and the International Labour Organization (ILO) are oriented more towards social goals and have a richer view of education. Of course, within the world of "transnational subpolitics," some such organizations have more global power and influence than others. Yet despite these differences, nowadays when international or transnational organizations of whatever sort write policy about education, their policy texts are almost inevitably intertwined with knowledge economy and other related narratives specifically and economics more generally. Indeed, the lines between education and economic policy are difficult to discern when it comes to the matter of the knowledge economy.

As King (2002, p. 312) observes, it has become "commonplace to attach the word knowledge to many different aspects of society and the economy." Indeed, the term "knowledge economy" is enmeshed in a plethora of related concepts with somewhat different meanings. In recent years many policymakers around the world have formed policy by fusing various ideas about the relationship between knowledge, information, learning, the economy and society. Policies have been developed around notions of the knowledge (-based, -driven) economy/society/revolution; the learning economy/society, and the information economy/society/age. They have included a range of related terms such as: knowledge assets/accumulation/workers/management; learning culture/city/organization; life-long learning; and innovation. Most policy documents contain a rather ambiguous blend of such concepts. Nonetheless— and despite this ambiguity—such terms have become powerful drivers and levers of education and other policies in the "community of states" and those transnational organizations that are our focus here. Let us now consider how the key concept "knowledge economy" is mobilized first within the OECD and then the World Bank and with what implications for the matters under scrutiny here.

*Knowledge Economy Policies for the "Developed" World: The Case of the OECD*

In 1996 OECD published its landmark document *The knowledge-based economy* (1996) and the concept of the knowledge economy defined in it provides the basis for most subsequent policy development in a number of educational fields.[1] According to this document,

The term *"knowledge-based economy"* results from a fuller recognition of the role of knowledge and technology in economic growth. Knowledge, as embodied in human beings (as *"human capital"*) and in technology, has always been central to economic development. But only over the last few years has its relative importance been recognised, just as that importance is growing. The OECD economies are more strongly dependent on the production, distribution and use of knowledge than ever before. (OECD, 1996, p. 9, italics in original)

It is clear that knowledge is being revalued as an economic resource, but, beyond this, how does this OECD document define knowledge?

At the same time as making reference to Gibbon's et al.'s theory of Mode 2 knowledge (see Bullen, Kenway & Robb, this volume), this document works with Lundvall's and Johnson's (1994) typology of knowledge: know-what, know-how, know-why and know-who. It begins by distinguishing knowledge from information, stating that:

Knowledge is a much broader concept than information, which is generally the *"know-what"* and *"know-why"* components of knowledge. These are also the types of knowledge which come closest to being market commodities or economic resources to be fitted into economic production functions. Other types of knowledge—particularly know-how and know-who—are more *"tacit knowledge"* and are more difficult to codify and measure. (OECD, 1996, p. 12, italics in original)

Know-what refers to knowledge of facts, know-why to rules, laws or principles. Know-how refers to knowledge acquired through practical experience. Know-who relates to knowledge about who knows what and who knows how to do it and so puts social relationships to the fore.

In the knowledge economy, the creation, diffusion and use of both tacit and codified knowledge are central. Indeed, "The determinants of success of enterprises, and of national economies as a whole, is [*sic*] ever more reliant upon their effectiveness in gathering and utilizing knowledge" (OECD, 1996, p. 14). In regard to know-what and know-why, this results in increased attention being paid to "distribution networks of knowledge," that is, information and communication technologies. In regard to know-how and know-who—those knowledges acquired through, and embedded in, social practice—this results in a focus on "National Systems of Innovation."[2] These entail "knowledge networks" consisting of national and international flows and interactions between industry, government and academia. In this context, "Strategic know-how and competence are being developed interactively and shared within subgroups and networks, where know-who is significant" (OECD, 1996, p. 14). Indeed, "the economy becomes a hierarchy of networks, driven by the acceleration in the rate of change and the rate of learning" (OECD, 1996, p. 14) and requires new roles to be played by the state and by the university.

## The Role of the State

The OECD is an advocate of state policy intervention, although this is not to be understood as state financial assistance, which is in decline. Globalization provides incentives for firms to innovate and compete and, in turn, it is the state's role to promote, coordinate and direct actors within the framework of a National Innovation System (NIS) "which support[s] the advance and use of knowledge in the economy" (OECD, 1996, p. 24). NIS frameworks will vary from country to country, but the OECD (2002, p. 8) suggests that "Innovation governance should be as flexible as possible, building upon a division of labor between public and private sectors."

"Innovation reposes on economy-wide knowledge flows" (2002, p. 13), and it is the task of governments to act as "catalysts and organizers" (2002, p. 55) of these flows. The state structures the innovation process by: enhancing firms' innovative capacities; exploiting the power of the market; securing investment in knowledge; promoting the commercialization of publicly-funded research; promoting cluster development; and promoting internationally-open networks. Further, the state takes an "active role" in the support of NIS infrastructure, via the provision of incentives for investment in training and R&D, and the promotion of education and training and firm-level organizational change. It likewise

> exert[s] a strong influence on the innovation process through the financing and steering of public organizations that are directly involved in knowledge generation and diffusion (universities, public labs), and through the provision of financial and regulatory incentives to all actors of the innovation system. (OECD, 2002, p. 3)

This new role the OECD envisages for the state in developed countries requires specific policy-making strategies. The OECD (2002, p. 11) recommends "a more horizontal approach" to policy making which combines "the efforts of several policy areas in dedicated interventions." In relation to conventional policy making, the NIS framework is seen as "adding value," enabling government "to promote innovation by integrating technology and innovation policy within the general framework of economic policy" (OECD, 2002, p. 10). Coordinating higher education policy within an economic framework leads to the subordination of other values to economic values as we will now show.

## The Role of the Tertiary Sector

According to the OECD (1996, p. 21), "A country's science system takes on increased importance in a knowledge-based economy," placing "Public research laboratories and institutions of higher education . . . at the core of the science system." Because this system "more broadly includes government science ministries and research councils, certain enterprises and other private bodies, and supporting infrastructure," the university is drawn tightly into the orbit of economic policy. Paradoxically, while this statement is about university science and science-related faculties, it is nonetheless now applied to universities as a whole. In other words, the basis of the state's increasingly interventionist role in higher education as a whole is its interest in a part of that whole: science and technology. Furthermore, at the same time as universities and research institutions are increasingly valued as producers of scientific and technological knowledge, they cannot presume to dominate knowledge production in a knowledge economy.

Here, the OECD (1996, p.22) points to Gibbons et al.'s (1994) contention that there is no "originating point for scientific knowledge" due to its massification and diffusion throughout society. It is also argued that science (new knowledge created through basic research) and technology (knowledge generated through applied or commercial research) are de-differentiating and "can be produced as joint products of the same research activity" (OECD, 1996, p. 22). As a consequence, universities are increasingly expected to conduct applied research and problem-solving activities in areas increasingly defined by industry and with commercial outcomes—in other words, they are expected to produce "exploitable knowledge." These developments have been assisted in part by the restructuring of research councils "to emphasise strategic areas, to promote synergies between disciplines and to involve the private sector" (OECD, 1996, p. 26), and in part by reductions in core public funding. Funding reductions have "encouraged universities and other publicly funded research organizations to enter this booming market, especially when they can build on already solid linkages with industry" (OECD, 2002, p. 33). These funding reductions have created the need for universities to "economize on resources and achieve the scale of benefits of joint activities" (p. 22), with "positive" outcomes such as increased international and industry collaboration.

Research increasingly functions along economic lines, but as the OECD notes, there are some impediments to this. These arise from within both the private and university sectors. For instance, much science is regarded as a "public good" and, as a result, there is a tendency for the private sector to under-invest in it. After all, the private sector will only invest in research from which it will profit. This means that while the state still has a role to play in supporting research for the public good, it may also mean that it might be "necessary to modify or reject the idea that science is a public good" (OECD, 1996, p. 22) if the economic potential of knowledge is to be fully exploited. The reluctance of the private sector to invest in research is intensified by resistance from some quarters of the university. The OECD notes the skepticism of some as to whether the private sector will fund "truly basic research" and fears about researcher autonomy. Having raised such concerns, the OECD fails to address the problem of how the state will resolve the tensions involved. How can it speak of state funding assistance for basic and public good research, but at the same time talk up the benefits of reducing state funding for universities and of transferring funding responsibilities to the market and industry?

Higher education policy for a knowledge economy entails further contradictions. At the same time as the transmission of knowledge is widely acknowledged to be equally important as knowledge production, there is an increasing gap between the university's research and teaching missions, raising new issues of the quality of teaching (OECD, 1996). The OECD acknowledges that industry funding may also be detrimental in terms of how universities specialize their research and in "steering overall research activity in a more commercial direction" (1996, p. 25). Moreover, the contribution of academe to knowledge production may "actually weaken under the burden of proving its economic relevance" (OECD, 1996, p. 25). Likewise, the report acknowledges the possibility that university/industry collaboration may act to concentrate the best researchers in a few universities or research centers, and so limit the ability of excluded institutions to provide the best teaching and research opportunities for their students. However, the OECD (1996, p. 25) concludes that "these concerns may be unfounded in light of the increasing ability for researchers to be linked electronically through information and communication technologies." This is a remarkably naïve notion and we seriously doubt that ICTs can address the complex issues involved.

## The OECD, the Humanities and the Knowledge Economy

This overview of OECD knowledge economy policy helps to explain the changing nature of the university. As a key contributor to any National Innovation System, the university is expected to adapt to the needs of industry and the needs of the state in terms of its overall economic policy. Hence the movement away from a model of the university in which research is the basis of teaching, to one in which research is the basis of commercial and entrepreneurial activities. This overview also helps to explain why science and technology have gained such an ascendant position within universities. Scientific knowledges are the most easily codified and are thus the most easily translated into economic outcomes.

While the arts and humanities typically work with knowledge codified in cultural texts—and, indeed, have embraced the task of codifying their knowledge in databases and so forth—it is not here that the most important aspect of its knowledge resides. Knowledge creation and transmission in the humanities is tacit, it resides in know-how, that is, the particular analytical, critical and aesthetic knowledge and skills that are the tools for working with codified knowledge. Of course, the sciences also entail tacit knowledge. They, too, require "Capabilities for selecting relevant and disregarding irrelevant information, recognizing patterns in information, interpreting and decoding information as well as learning new and forgetting old skills are in increasing demand" (OECD, 1996, p. 13). However, humanities knowledge is socially embedded in ways that scientific knowledge, by and large, is not. Scientific knowledge is favored over humanities knowledge because, on the one hand, it is the most amenable to codification, and on the other hand, because its "codification, standardization and normalization" increases the rate of innovation and so economic growth (Lundvall, 1998, p. 9). It is precisely the standardization and normalization of knowledge that the humanities so often seek to disrupt.

### Knowledge Economy Policies for the "Developing" World: The Case of the World Bank

Knowledge economy narratives are inflected somewhat differently for the so-called developing world. The World Bank, for example, has commenced a three-year program to address the implications of the knowledge economy in developing countries. *Education for the Knowledge Economy* (2002) builds on the World Bank's 1998–1999 World Development Report, *Knowledge for Development* (1999). World Bank policies embrace the OECD notion that knowledge is the key to economic and, indeed, social progress and their concern is to identify the key features of the knowledge economy so that developing nations can integrate into a global knowledge-based economy and also reduce poverty. World Bank policy is based on supporting the development of four key "pillars" of the knowledge economy:

- A supportive economic and institutional regime to provide incentives for the efficient use of existing and new knowledge and the flourishing of entrepreneurship,
- An educated and skilled population to create, share, and use knowledge,
- A dynamic information infrastructure to facilitate the effective communication, dissemination, and processing of information,

- An efficient innovation system of firms, research centers, universities, consultants, and other organizations to tap into the growing stock of global knowledge, assimilate and adapt it to local needs, and create new knowledge. (World Bank, 2002a, p. 2; see also 2002c, pp. 5–6)

What are the implications of these policy goals for the roles of the state and the tertiary sector, and what impact might they have on the humanities in developing nations?

## The Role of the State

When it comes to developing nations and the knowledge economy, the World Bank does not advocate a minimalist role for the state (see, for example, World Bank, 2002c, p. 11). Following the OECD, the World Bank argues that the primary roles of the state in the knowledge economy involve establishing a coherent policy framework (usually associated with national innovation systems, science and technology and ICTs); setting an enabling regulatory environment; and offering appropriate financial incentives (World Bank, 2002b, p. 63). As *Constructing Knowledge Societies* (World Bank, 2002b, p. 6) puts it:

> The state has a responsibility to put in place an enabling framework that encourages tertiary education institutions to be more innovative and responsive to the needs of a globally competitive knowledge economy and the changing labor market requirements for advanced human capital.

Setting an enabling regulatory environment refers to governments encouraging competition amongst education providers and encouraging foreign investment, particularly for those countries that have a small tertiary sector and few funds to invest. Unlike governments of OECD nations, governments of developing nations, it is argued, should finance basic education where private investment is not currently rewarded, and largely withdraw from financing tertiary and continuing education (those education sectors where private bodies can profit), except where there is a need to subsidize disadvantaged students.

The role of the state is to continue to fund primary and secondary education. Governments need, therefore, to stimulate private investment in higher education, as well as investment from international development organizations such as the World Bank. Such organizations can assist with such large capital expenditures as ICTs, partner and facilitate private investment in tertiary education, and create the conditions for competition, investment, and trade. The role of the state is to ensure the smooth running of a competitive and profitable private sector in those sectors of education that have the potential for profitability. The report on *Lifelong Learning* (World Bank, 2002a, p. 61) suggests further that governments in developing nations should consider providing education through the private sector, distance learning, and on-line delivery, as well as re-allocating recourses away from tertiary education to secondary education. More generally, the World Bank argues that regulatory environment should maximize learner choice, institutional autonomy and competition, and student access. Offering appropriate financial incentives refers to governments developing competitive funding mechanisms, encourage funding diversification through, for example, industry collaboration, and the development for learners/students of a mix of financing instruments (cost recovery, subsidies, and incentives).

Although the World Bank stresses the necessity of liberalization and private investment and global trade in education services, it notes certain inadequacies in the market that the state needs to attend to so that an education market can freely and efficiently operate:

> While often beneficial, the rise of market forces can have adverse consequences, illustrating the danger of unbridled competition without adequate regulatory and compensatory mechanisms. From an equity perspective, firstly, increased institutional choice for students is meaningful only for those who can afford to pay tuition at private institutions or for those who have access to financial aid. . . . Secondly, when funding disparities among institutions are too large, it becomes increasingly difficult to maintain competition on equal terms, even in high-income countries. (World Bank, 2002b, pp. 52–3)

The state is therefore required to develop a coherent innovation system and to even out any disparities that may hamper the efficient operation of a competitive higher education system (largely through regularly frameworks and student loans). The policy trajectory for developing nations encourages them to open up their education market to international education providers (both corporeal and virtual) and to regulate these bodies using internationally agreed-upon standards. A consistent theme in World Bank policy is that, for developing nations to compete in the global knowledge economy, the state must concentrate its limited financial investments in primary and secondary education, regulate market-driven competition in the tertiary sector, and link these regulations to a national innovation system.

## The Role of the Tertiary Sector

For the World Bank, education is a key factor in a knowledge economy, but it can only be valuable when it is tied to an overall innovation plan, when it accommodates the interests of industry both in terms of content and mode of delivery, and when it is funded in a way that maximizes competition (and hence the opportunities for investment and private gain), and the social good. World Bank policy claims that there are three primary roles for tertiary education in a knowledge economy: (1) to support a national innovation system (2) human capital formation and (3) nation building, democracy and social cohesion (World Bank, 2002b).

First, according to World Bank policies tertiary institutions need to see themselves as key participants within an innovation system rather than as entities unto themselves, producing basic research. They need to be involved in an ongoing dialogue between industry, community and the state. In a knowledge economy, the argument goes, knowledge production will occur across a diversity of sites, in industry, the community, and education institutions, and none of these can ignore the imperative of innovation:

> Continuous, market-driven innovation is the key to competitiveness, and thus to economic growth, in the knowledge economy. This requires not only a strong science and technology base, but, just as importantly, the capacity to link fundamental and applied research; to convert the results of that research to new products, services, processes, or materials; and to bring these innovations quickly to market. It also entails an ability to tap into and participate in regional and global networks of research and innovation. (World Bank, 2002c, p. 21)

Indeed *Building Knowledge Economies* (World Bank, 2002c, p. 22) suggests that all research institutions need to assess and rationalize their research capabilities in light of their ability to contribute to a national innovation system. The policy trajectory here is towards science and technology, research that has an obvious commercial potential, and integrating research with industry goals.

Second, tertiary education should attend to human capital formation, that is, the development of creative and flexible workers who can constantly adapt to the changing demands of a knowledge-based economy (World Bank, 2002b, p. 14). A key to human capital formation is lifelong learning. This requires institutions to develop in the learner decision-making, problem-solving, pedagogical, and reflective skills—as opposed to task-specific skills—throughout the life cycle of the learner (World Bank, 2002a, p. 2). For learners being successful in the knowledge economy requires:

. . . mastering a new set of knowledge and competencies. These include basic academic skills, such as literacy, foreign language, math and science skills, and the ability to use information and communication technology. Workers must be able to use these skills effectively, act autonomously and reflectively, and join and function in socially heterogeneous groups. (World Bank, 2002a, p. x)

The keyword here is flexibility and likewise the tertiary education system itself must become more flexible in terms of format, subjects and lifelong learning opportunities.

Third, according to the World Bank tertiary education in a knowledge economy needs to assist in the development of socially cohesive institutions and networks in "developing" countries. The university is to inculcate democratic and local cultural values through the humanities and social sciences. Clearly there is an acknowledgement here that higher education policy needs to attend to more than science and technology. *Constructing Knowledge Societies* (World Bank, 2002b, p. 18), for example, states that:

A meaningful education for the 21st century should stimulate all aspects of human intellectual potential. It should not simply emphasize access to global knowledge in science and management, but it should also uphold the richness of local cultures and values, supported by time-honored and eternally valuable disciplines of the humanities and social sciences such as philosophy, literature, and arts.

Indeed, *Constructing Knowledge Societies* (2002b, p. 31) argues that the humanities and social sciences are crucial to the stability of a political and economic order whether that be a knowledge-based society and economy or not:

Through the transmission of democratic values and cultural norms, tertiary education contributes to the promotion of civic behaviors, nation building, and social cohesion. This, in turn, supports the construction and strengthening of social capital. . . . The institutions, relationships, and norms that emerge from tertiary education are instrumental in influencing the quality of a society's interactions, which underpin economic, political, and social development. Universities and other tertiary institutions are the crossroads for social cooperation, which can foster strong networks, stimulate voluntary activity, and promote extra curricular learning and innovation. A growing body of research supports the notion that the general quality of social infrastructure is a critical factor in the effectiveness of governments, institutions, and firms . . .

This emphasis on a broad role for the university and on the importance of the humanities and social sciences to a knowledge economy/society is a significant departure from OECD policy and it is intriguing to consider why this is the case.

## The World Bank, the Humanities and the Knowledge Economy

The World Bank policy trajectory is fraught with contradictions. It is exerting pressure on developing nations to privatize their higher education services and to open them up to international competition. They are also to prioritize science and technology, industry collaboration and commercialization goals for research. Further, they are to develop curriculum suitable to constructing globally inflected entrepreneurial subjects. However, on the other hand they are to emphasize the importance of the arts, humanities and, indeed, the social sciences in inculcating civic values and social cohesion rooted in local values and traditions. Interestingly, science here is implicitly seen as global and the arts and humanities, as well as the social sciences, as local.

In this scenario the state becomes in effect a site of struggle between international bodies over the direction of education policy and over the question of whether education and knowledge is a commodity for economic goals, or a public good to facilitate local knowledges and social cohesion. Tertiary education in this scenario seems to be weighed down with the contradictory needs of global capital expansion and local cultural and social needs. And, the latter are only seen as important to the extent that they support the former. The pressure on the humanities is to function successfully within a global knowledge economy and also to maintain a local value system and support indigenous culture. It is noteworthy that the World Bank has begun to articulate both a willingness to support the humanities and social sciences in developing nations and to acknowledge their importance to the ongoing viability of a knowledge economy. It thus offers them a value and status that is missing in key OECD policies. However, the extent to which a privately and internationally funded tertiary sector will support social and cultural knowledge that is indigenous and directed toward the local public good remains an open question. As noted above, in the context of developed national economies, the OECD has indicated its concerns about such matters and about the future of basic research and the autonomy of university research. Such matters are even more pressing for developing nations which, on the advice of the World Bank, may have no home-grown university sector to address specific local needs and concerns.

### Conclusion

As the chapters throughout this book indicate, knowledge economy policies have raised some profound issues for the future of the arts and humanities in the academy. For some writers, this policy moment provides exciting new opportunities to certain sectors of the arts and humanities to demonstrate their contemporary relevance, their potential to partner in new ways and to produce "exploitable knowledge." Others have expressed serious disquiet about the hegemony of the sciences and the notion of "exploitable knowledge" and its implications for those sectors of the arts and humanities that are not amenable to commercialization. Collectively these chapters point to the dangerous opportunities that knowledge economies provide. Further, most chapters adopt national foci and "first world" sensibilities. Yet, as we have suggested throughout this chapter, the issues and politics here are global. The "community of states" is divided between those states with developed economies that belong to the OECD and who collectively make policy that informs other policies for the rest of "the community," including states with developing economies. While the arts and humanities in "First World" universities certainly have their problems, these pale in significance when compared to those faced by "Third World" arts and humanities scholarship. Indeed, if the World Bank has its way, which it usually does, it is likely that the First World universities will be exporting education to developing countries, thus undermining indigenous arts and humanities and also the growth of local universities. This is a sober note to end on, but it is important that this be seen as a global phenomenon with different implications for developed and developing countries. The notion of exploitable knowledge takes on another meaning in this context.

## Notes

1. For instance, equipping individuals for participation in the knowledge-based economy—or knowledge society and the new learning economy—is an explicit aim of OECD Education Directorate publications relating to lifelong learning (2001a), information and communication technologies (2001b) and school management (2001c).
2. The OECD has put much effort into providing a "sound conceptual framework and an empirical basis" for governments "to assess how the contribution of public policy to national innovation performance could be improved" (2002, p. 3). For instance, *Dynamising national innovation systems* (2002), builds on seven years of research and a number of previous publications (see for example, OECD 1999a, 1999b, 2001).

## References

Beck, U. (1997). *What is globalisation?* Cambridge: Polity.
Currie, J. & Newson, J. (eds) (1998). *Universities and globalization: Critical perspectives.* Thousand Oaks, CA.: Sage.

Gibbons, M., Limoges, C., Nowotny, H., Schwartzman, S, Scott, P., & Trow, M. (1994). *The new production of knowledge: The dynamics of science and research in contemporary societies.* London: Sage.

Held, D. & McGrew, A. (2002). *Globalization/Anti-globalization.* Cambridge, UK: Polity.

Henry, M., Lingard, B., Rizvi, F., & Taylor, S. (2001). *The OECD, globalisation and education policy*, Oxford, UK: Elsevier-Pergamon.

King, K. (2002). Banking on knowledge: The new knowledge projects of the World Bank. *Compare, 32* (3), 311–326.

Lundvall, B.-Å. (1998) The learning economy—implications for the knowledge base of health and education systems. Paper presented at the Paper presented at the High-Level Seminar on Production, Mediation and Use of Knowledge in the Education and Health Sectors, Paris, 14–15 May.

Lundvall, B.-Å. & Johnson, B. (1994). The learning economy. *Journal of Industry Studies*, 1 (2), 23–42.

Organization for Economic Cooperation and Development (2002). *Dynamising national innovation systems.* Paris: OECD.

———. (2001a). *Investing in competencies for all*, OECD: Paris.

———. (2001b). *Learning to change: ICT in schools*, OECD: Paris.

———. (2001c).*Teachers for tomorrow's schools*, OECD: Paris.

———. (2001). *Innovative clusters: Drivers of national innovation systems.* Paris: OECD.

———. (1999a). *Managing national innovation systems.* Paris: OECD.

———. (1999b). *Boosting innovation: The cluster approach.* Paris: OECD.

———. (1996). *The knowledge-based economy.* Paris: OECD.

Stromquist, N. & Monkman, K. (eds) (2000). *Globalization and education: Integration and contestation across cultures.* Lanham, MD: Rowman & Littlefield.

Tomlinson, J. (1999) *Globalisation and culture.* Cambridge: Polity.

World Bank (2002a). *Lifelong learning in the global knowledge economy: Challenges for developing countries*, available online http://www1.worldbank.org/education/lifelong_learning/publications/Lifelong%20Learning_GKE.pdf

———. (2002b). *Constructing knowledge societies: New challenges for tertiary education. A World Bank report.* Education Group Human Development Network, available online http://www1.worldbank.org/education/pdf/Constructing%20Knowledge%20Societies.pdf

———. (2002c). *Building knowledge economies: Opportunities and challenges for EU accession countries. Final report of the Knowledge Economy Forum*, "Using Knowledge for Development in EU Accession Countries," available online http://lnweb18.worldbank.org/ECA/ECSSD.nsf/a3b026a6ee1e272585256ad2007130d3/9e9735587b22d64285256bcee05ddbad/$FILE/Building%20Knowledge%20 Economies-final%20final.pdf

———. (1999). *World Development Report: Knowledge for Development.* Washington, DC: World Bank.

# LIST OF CONTRIBUTORS

**Chika Anyanwu** is the Program Convenor for the Bachelor of Media, School of Humanities, University of Adelaide. His research interests include new media technology and the socio-cultural implications of changing media landscape; African cinema and media management; policy and regulation in developing world media.

**Elizabeth Bullen** is a Research Fellow in the School of Education, Monash University, Victoria, Australia. She has a Ph.D. in Australian Literature from Flinders University and is currently a research team member of the ARC "Knowledge Economy Project." Her research interests include gender, globalization, and consumption practices. She is co-author with Jane Kenway of *Consuming Children: Education-Advertising-Entertainment* (Open University Press, 2001).

**Stuart Cunningham** is Professor and Director of the Creative Industries Research and Applications Centre (CIRAC), Queensland University of Technology. His research and research management is in the fields of media, communications, cultural policy, higher education and in the "creative industries." His publications include *Framing Culture, Floating Lives: The Media and Asian Diasporas*, with John Sinclair; two major international studies for DEETYA/DETYA/DEST on "borderless" education and its implications for Australian higher and further education; and the textbooks *The Australian TV Book* and *The Media and Communications in Australia* (with Graeme Turner). He was co-author of the recent Australian Broadcasting Authority report, *The Future for Local Content? Options for Emerging Technologies*.

**Greg Hainge** is a Lecturer in French Studies, School of Humanities, University of Adelaide. His research interests include: the writing of Louis-Ferdinand Céline; muzak, pop, and contemporary electronic music. His publications include *Capitalism and Schizophrenia in the Later Novels of Louis-Ferdinand Céline; D'un . . . L'autre* and *(Post) noise: Contemporary Modes of Acoustic Expression and their Relationship to Culture and Analysis* (in press).

**Paul Jeffcutt** is Professor of Management Knowledge in the School of Management and Economics of Queen's University, Belfast. He is the founding Director of the University's Centre for Creative Industry and the founding Chair of the UK/Irish Creative Industries Research & Development Network (supported by the Royal Irish Academy, the British Council and NESTA). His research interests concern the interdisciplinary field and changing practices of management knowledge, concentrating on knowledge dynamics in the organization and management of creativity and innovation. He is the author of over 60 research publications and has held guest editorships with a range of international academic journals.

**Jane Kenway** is Professor of Education at Monash University, Victoria, Australia. Her research expertise is in the field of education policy and in sociology of education with reference to education systems in the context of wider social and cultural change. She is author of seven books and has published widely in edited collections and journals.

**Steve Loo** is a Senior Lecturer and Program Director (Architecture), Louis Laybourne-Smith School of Architecture and Design, University of South Australia. His research interests include the relationship between architectural production and theoretical work, application of twentieth century philosophy in architectural theory, and issues in the history and theory of technology surrounding digital technology and new media, information theory, and architectural representation.

**Susan Luckman** is a Lecturer in Communication Studies, School of Communication, Information and New Media, University of South Australia. Her research interests include the socio-cultural implications of new technologies; youth cultures and society; music technologies, sound, and cultural change; and cultural policy and social space.

**Stuart Macintyre** is Ernest Scott Professor of History, Dean of Arts and Professor Laureate at the University of Melbourne. He is Chair of the Humanities and Creative Arts Expert Advisory Committee to the Australian Research

Council. His books include *A Colonial Liberalism; A History for a Nation; The Oxford History of Australia, Vol. 4; The Reds: The Communist Party of Australia from Origins to Illegality;* and most recently, *The History Wars* (Melbourne University Press, 2003) with Anna Clark.

**Emily Potter** has completed a Ph.D. in English Studies at Adelaide University. Her research interests are in land and landscape in contemporary Australian fiction. She is currently involved with the public art project, *Tracks*, designed by Paul Carter, which attempts to "track" alternate voices and stories out of the official and exclusionary public and institutional space of North Terrace, Adelaide, South Australia.

**Sarah Redshaw** is Director of the Driving Cultures program at the Centre for Cultural Research, University of Western Sydney. She is a current postdoctoral research fellow with "Transforming Drivers: Driving as Social, Cultural and Gendered Practice," an innovative project which introduces a cultural approach to driver education. This is funded by the Australian Research Council and the NRMA Motoring and Services. Her research interests are in Spinozistic ethics; cultural studies and social, cultural and interpersonal relations.

**Simon Robb** is a Research Fellow in the School of Education, Monash University, Victoria, Australia. He is currently a researcher with the ARC "Knowledge Economy Project." His research interests include representations of cultural trauma, fictocriticism and local historical narratives. He has published with the Electronic Writing Research Ensemble and is the author of the ficto-critical novel *The Hulk* (Post Taste, 2003).

**Linda Marie Walker** is a Lecturer at the Louis Laybourne-Smith School of Architecture and Design, University of South Australia. Her research interests are in writing as design; language-based writing; the body as/in space; abandonment and ruined space; contemporary Australian visual arts and artists and curatorial practices. She is author of the novella, *The Woman, Mistaken* (Little Esther Books, 1999).

# INDEX

# ERUPTIONS
## New Thinking across the Disciplines

Erica McWilliam
*General Editor*

This is a series of red-hot women's writing after the "isms." It focuses on new cultural assemblages that are emerging from the de-formation, breakout, ebullience, and discomfort of postmodern feminism. The series brings together a post-foundational generation of women's writing that, while still respectful of the idea of situated knowledge, does not rely on neat disciplinary distinctions and stable political coalitions. This writing transcends some of the more awkward textual performances of a first generation of "feminism-meets-postmodernism" scholarship. It has come to terms with its own body of knowledge as shifty, inflammatory, and ungovernable.

The aim of the series is to make this cutting edge thinking more readily available to undergraduate and postgraduate students, researchers and new academics, and professional bodies and practitioners. Thus, we seek contributions from writers whose unruly scholastic projects are expressed in texts that are accessible and seductive to a wider academic readership.

Proposals and/or manuscripts are invited from the domains of: "post" humanities, human movement studies, sexualities, media studies, literary criticism, information technologies, history of ideas, performing arts, gay and lesbian studies, cultural studies, post-colonial studies, pedagogics, social psychology, and the philosophy of science. We are particularly interested in publishing research and scholarship with international appeal from Australia, New Zealand, and the United Kingdom.

For further information about the series and for the submission of manuscripts, please contact:

Erica McWilliam
Faculty of Education
Queensland University of Technology
Victoria Park Rd., Kelvin Grove Q 4059
Australia

To order other books in this series, please contact our Customer Service Department at:

(800) 770-LANG (within the U.S.)
(212) 647-7706 (outside the U.S.)
(212) 647-7707 FAX

Or browse online by series at:

www.peterlangusa.com